Animals Fart, TOO!

Color By Numbers for Kids

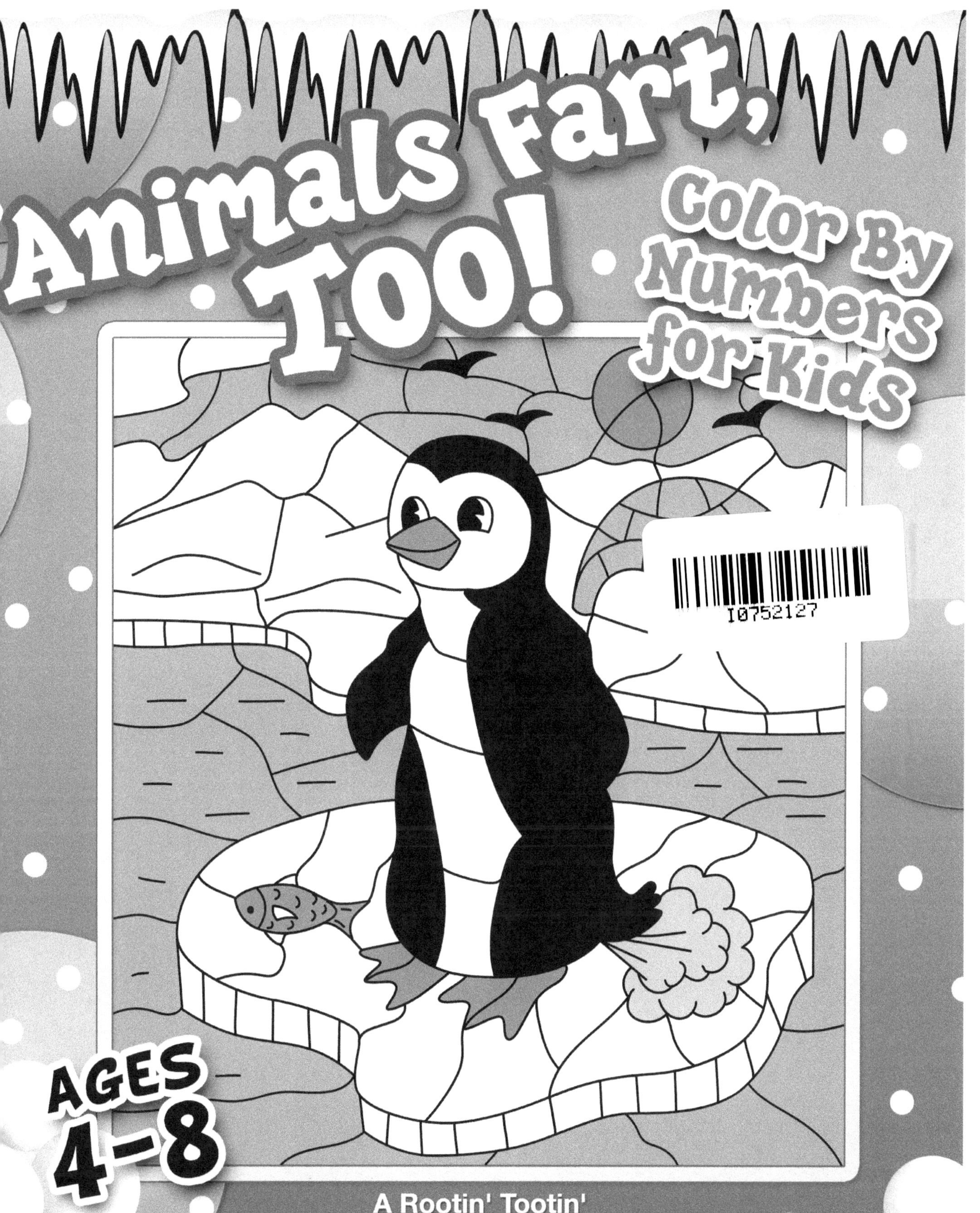

AGES 4-8

A Rootin' Tootin'
Farting Animal Coloring Book for Kids

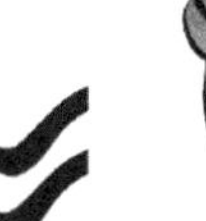
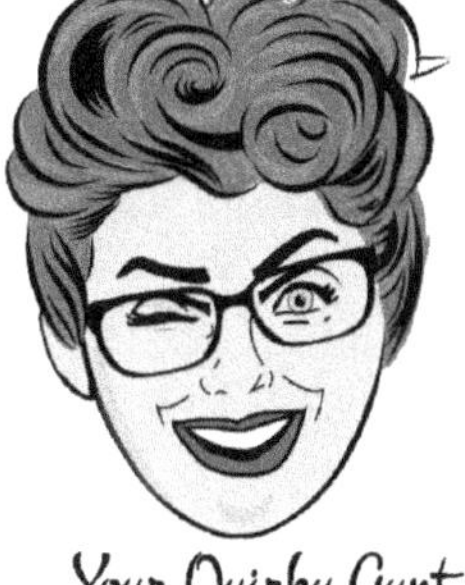

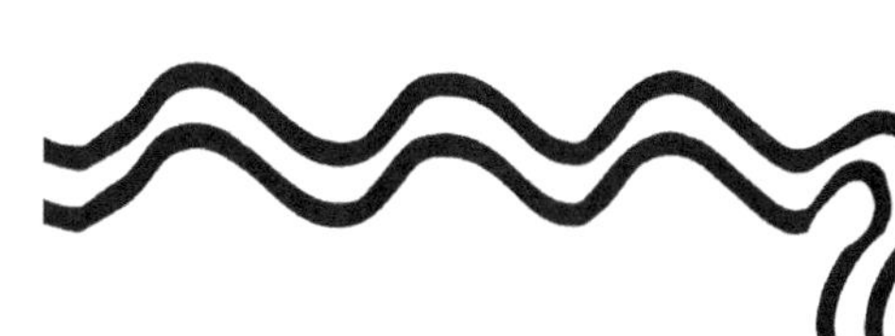

HI THERE!

YOUR QUIRKY AUNT WOULD LIKE TO THANK YOU FOR TAKING THE TIME TO BUY AND READ MY BOOK! I HOPE YOU ENJOY IT AS MUCH AS I DID WHEN CREATING IT! FUNNY IDEAS AND A RELAXED ENVIRONMENT ARE WHERE I DO MY BEST AND HOPE MY BOOKS DO JUST THAT FOR YOU AND YOUR KIDDOS! TO SAY THANK YOU FOR SUPPORTING MY QUIRKY IDEAS, I WANT TO GIVE AWAY A $50 AMAZON GIFT CARD TO AN AMAZON CUSTOMER MONTHLY!

EMAIL US FOR A CHANCE TO WIN OUR MONTHLY

**** $50 AMAZON GIFT CARD ****

IT'S SUPER EASY - EMAIL US AT YOURQUIRKYAUNT@GMAIL.COM AND PLEASE INCLUDE:

1. YOUR NAME
2. FEEBACK ABOUT THE BOOK (POSITIVE OR NEGATIVE)

LOOK FORWARD TO ALL YOUR COMMENTS AND THANK YOU AGAIN FOR YOUR SUPPORT!

STAY AWESOME,

YOUR QUIRKY AUNT

Follow Us on Facebook:
Your Quirky Aunt

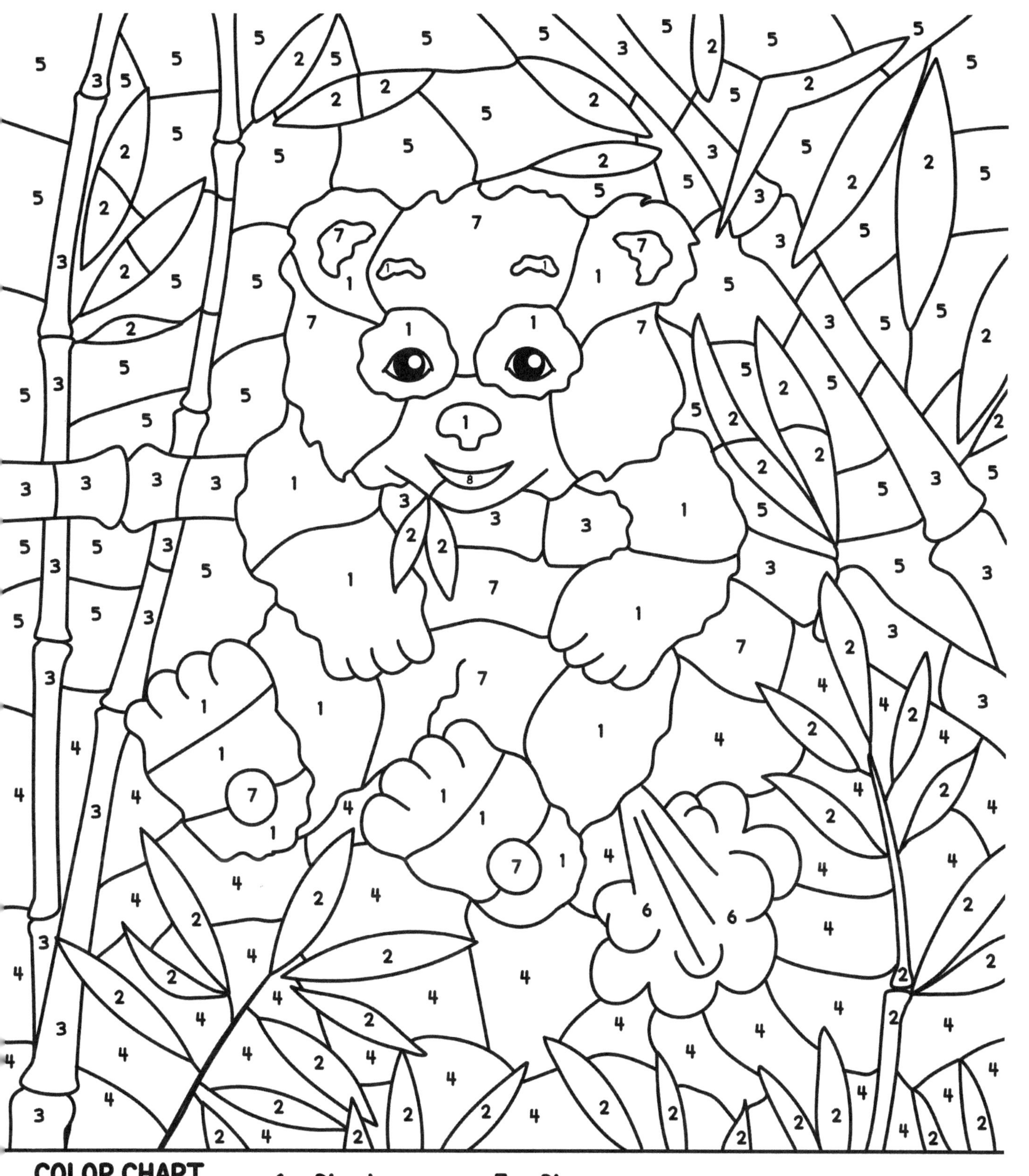

COLOR CHART

1 – Black	5 – Blue
2 – Green	6 – Gray
3 – Yellow	7 – White
4 – Brown	8 – Red

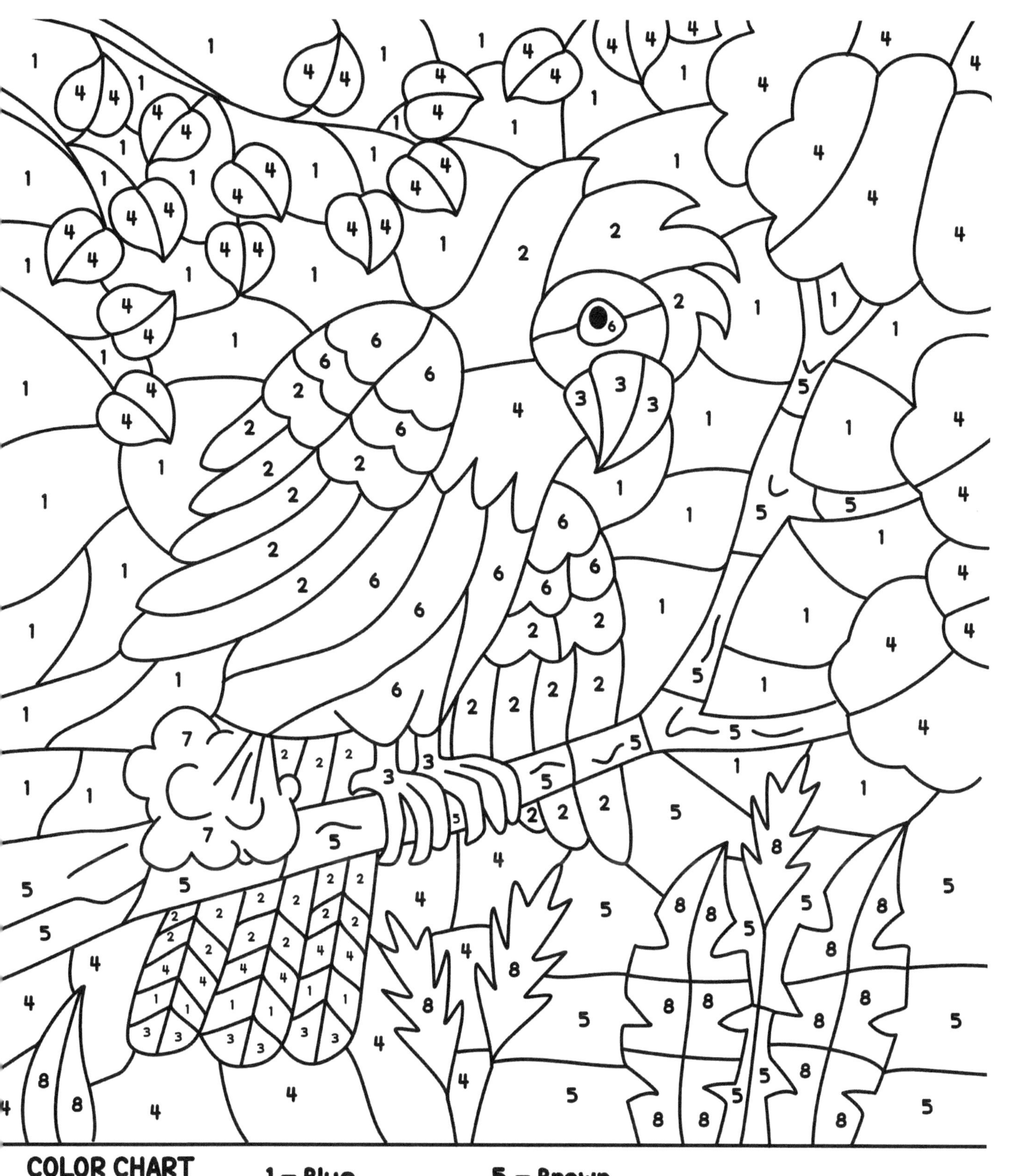

COLOR CHART

1 – Blue
2 – Red
3 – Orange
4 – Green
5 – Brown
6 – Yellow
7 – Gray
8 – Dark Green

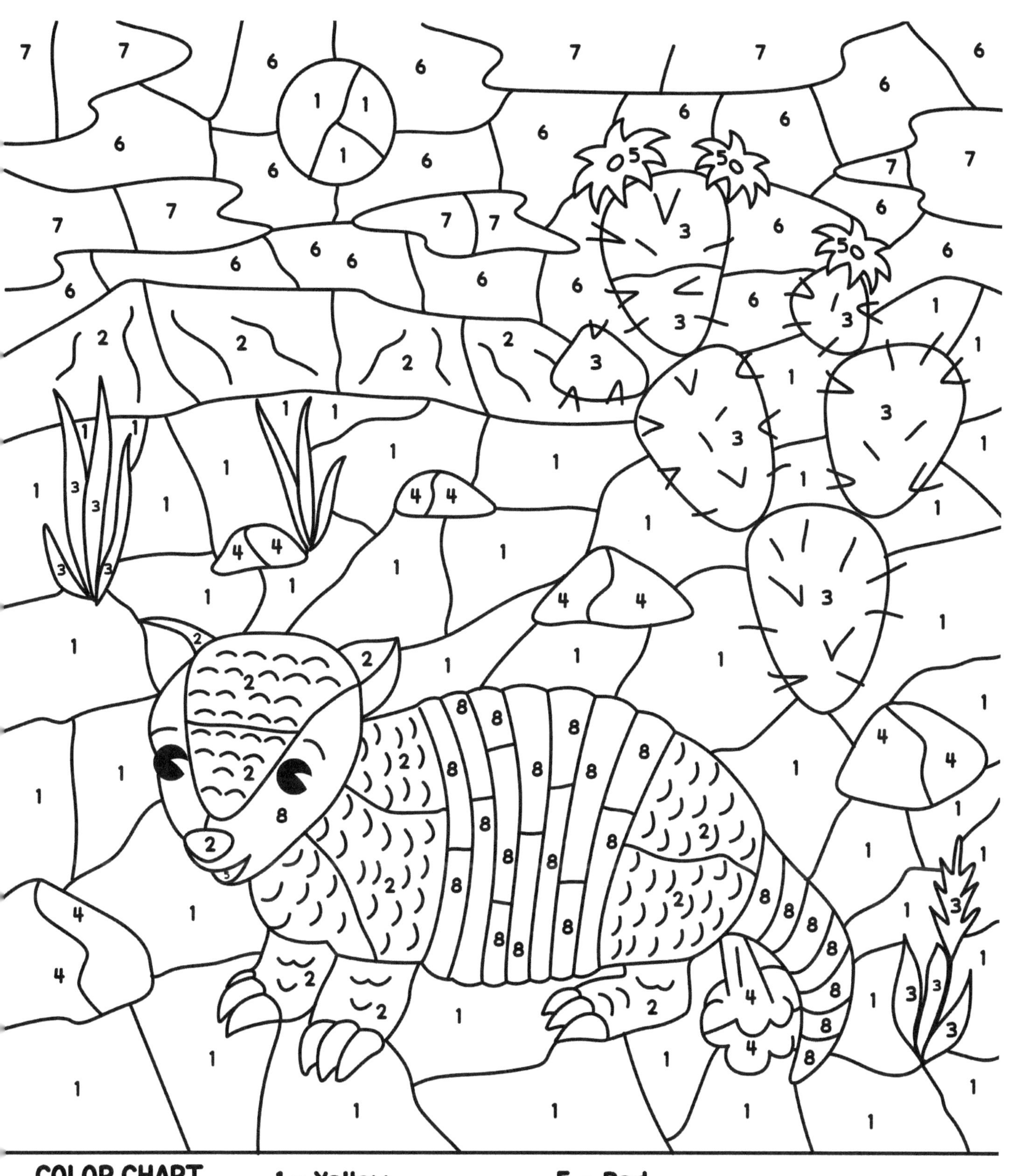

COLOR CHART

1 – Yellow
2 – Brown
3 – Green
4 – Gray
5 – Red
6 – Blue
7 – White
8 – Light Brown

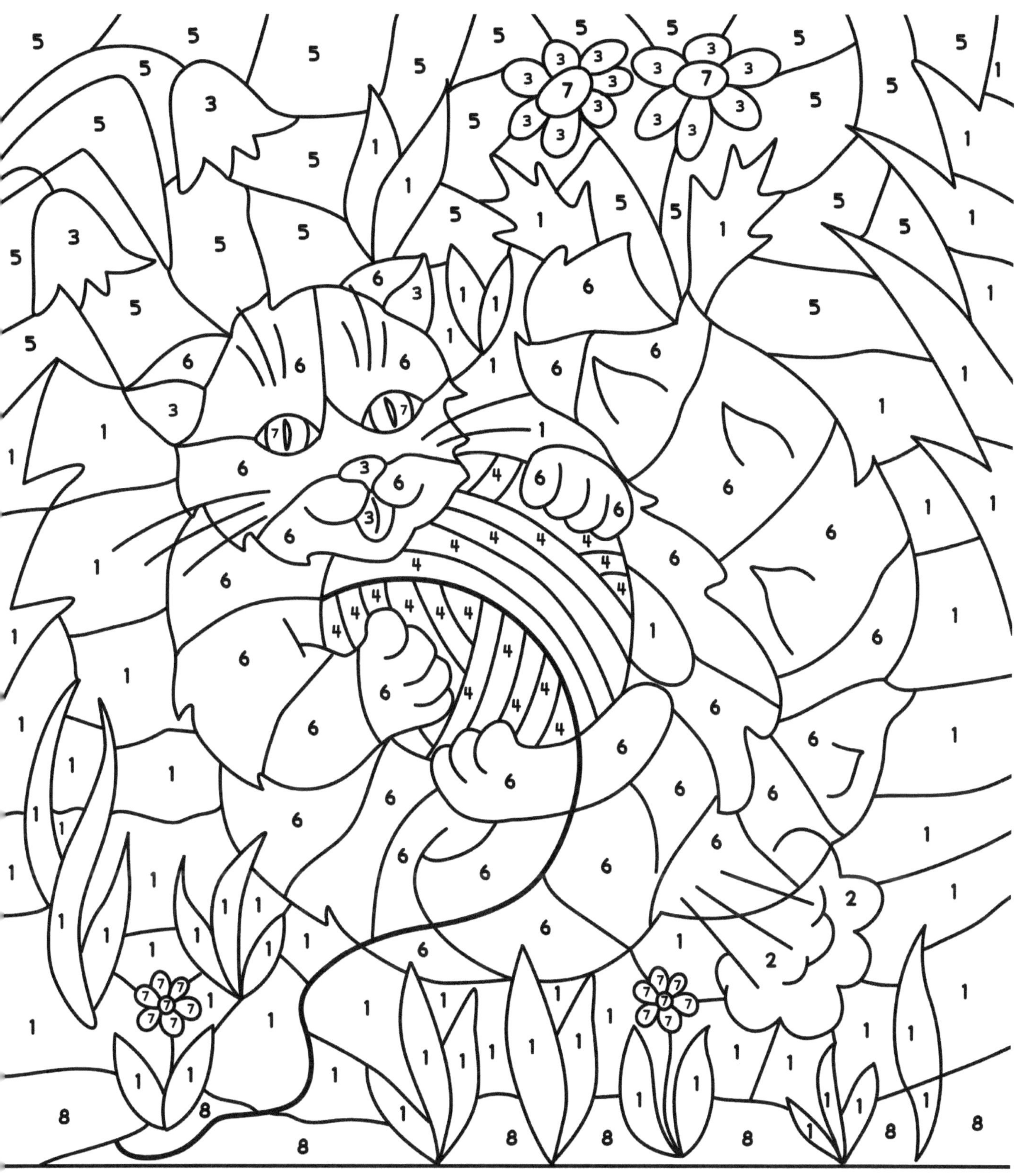

COLOR CHART

1 – Green
2 – Gray
3 – Pink
4 – Red
5 – Blue
6 – Orange
7 – Yellow
8 – Brown

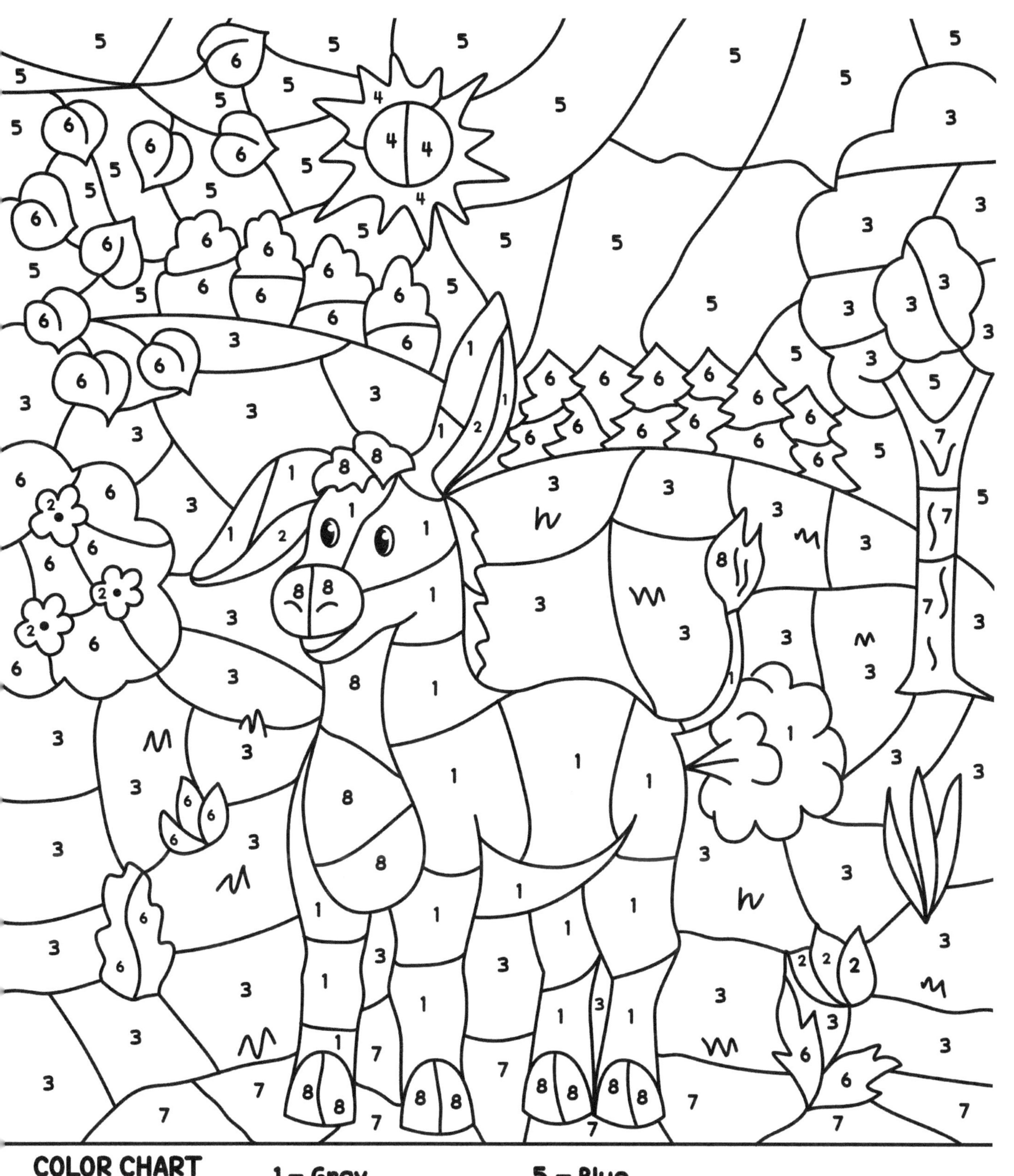

COLOR CHART

1 – Gray
2 – Pink
3 – Green
4 – Yellow
5 – Blue
6 – Dark Green
7 – Brown
8 – Charcoal

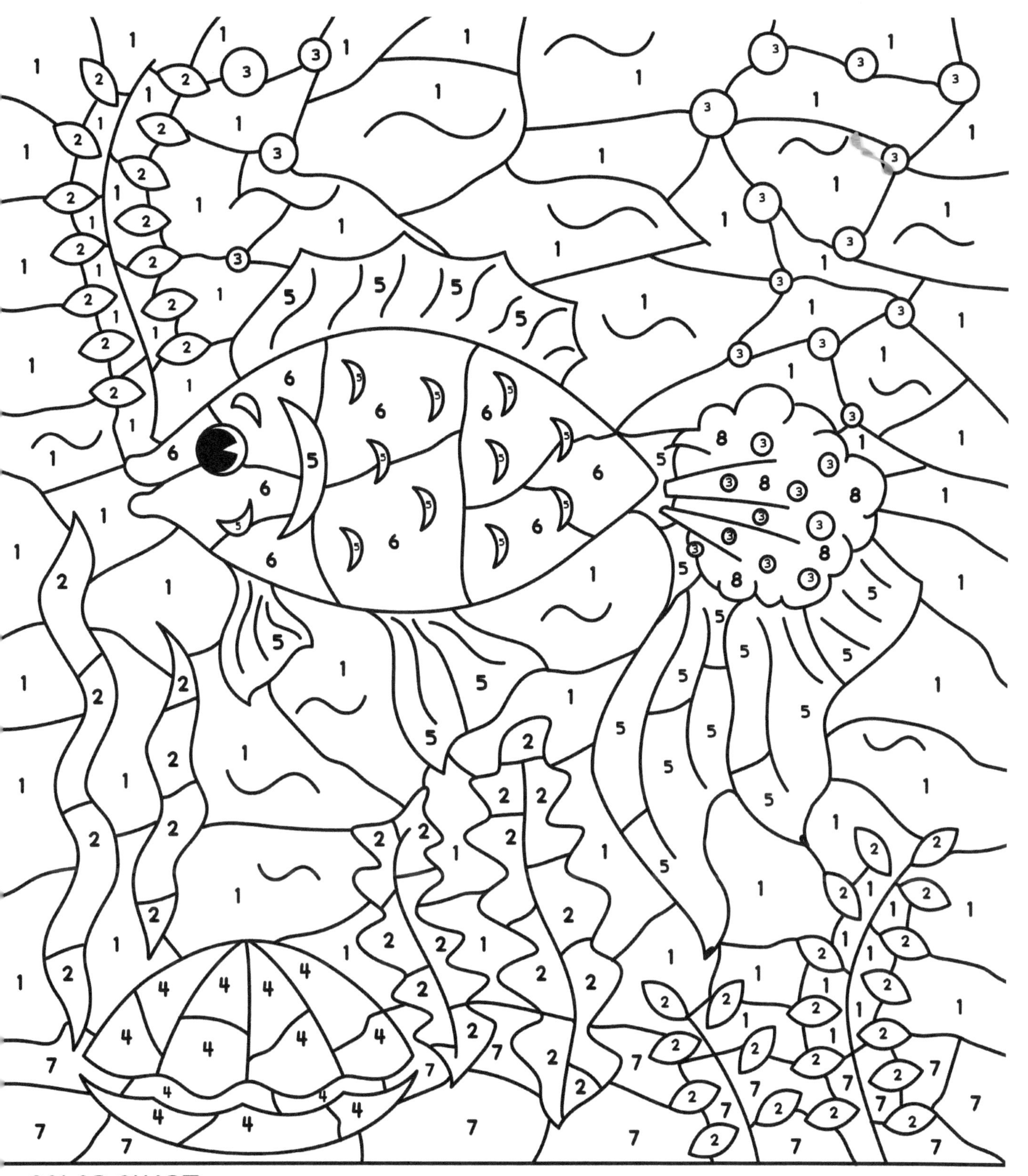

COLOR CHART

1 – Blue
2 – Green
3 – White
4 – Pink
5 – Purple
6 – Orange
7 – Tan
8 – Gray

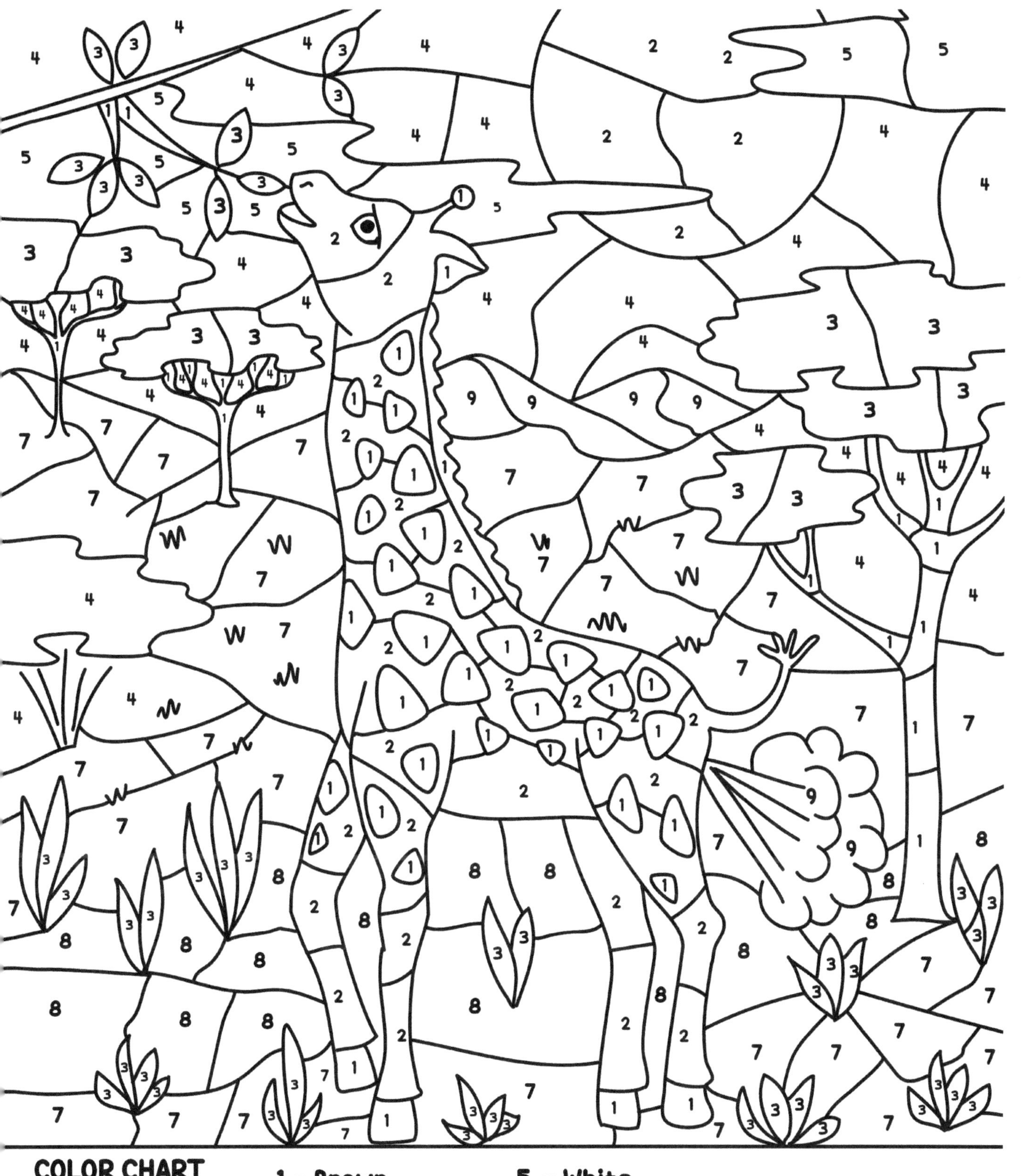

COLOR CHART

1 – Brown
2 – Yellow
3 – Dark Green
4 – Blue
5 – White
6 – Gray
7 – Green
8 – Orange

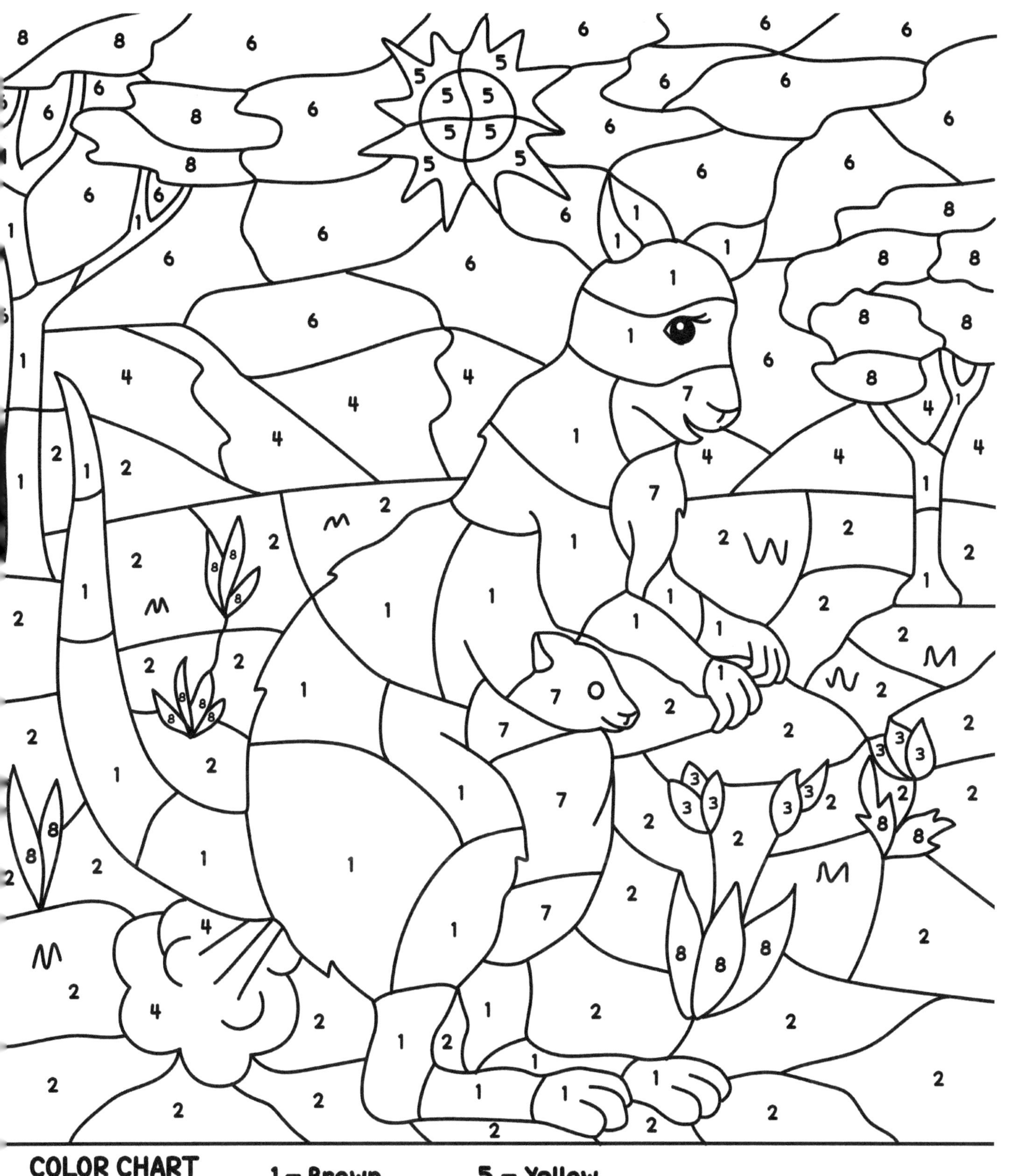

COLOR CHART

1 – Brown
2 – Green
3 – Purple
4 – Gray
5 – Yellow
6 – Blue
7 – Tan
8 – Dark Green

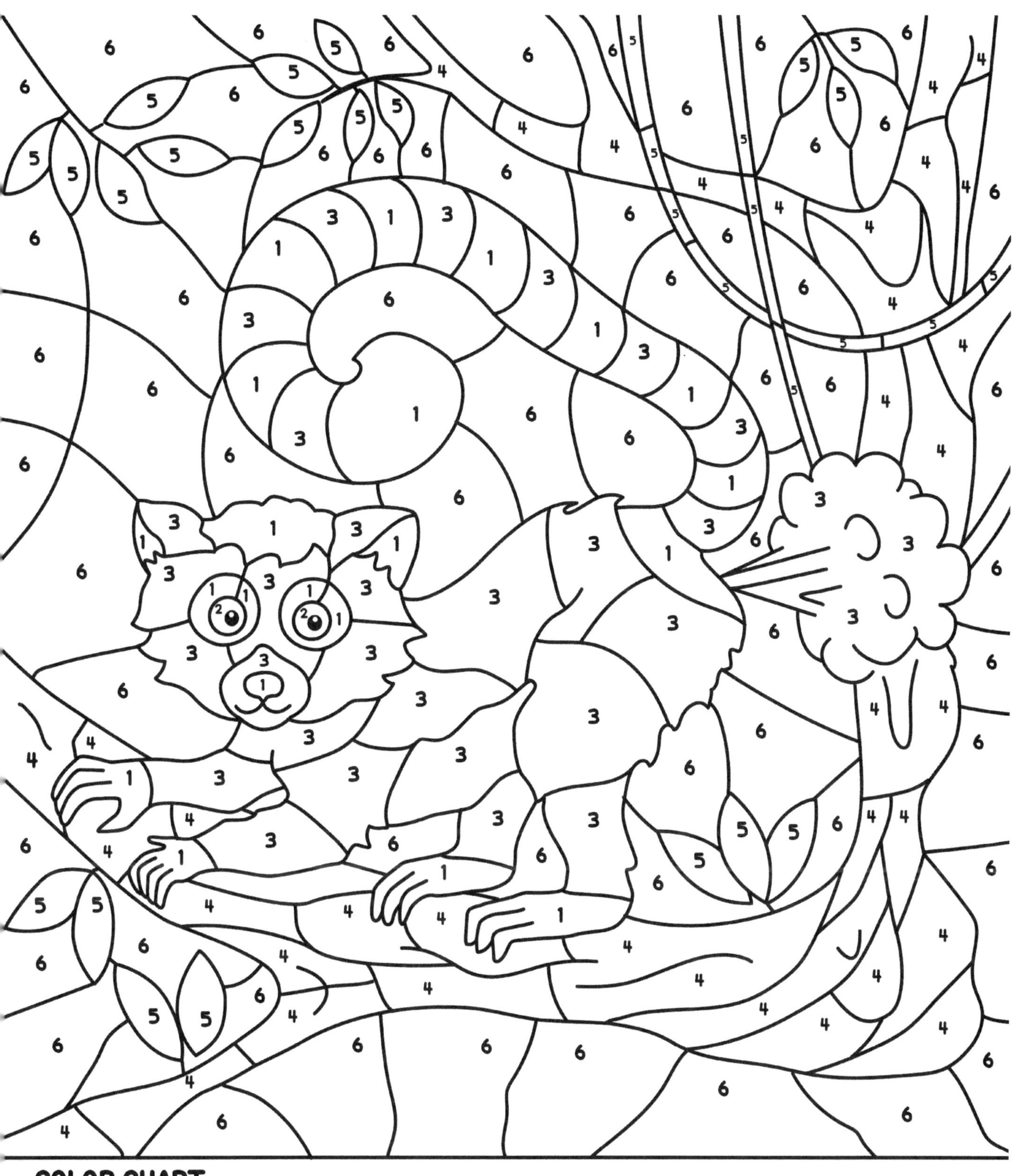

COLOR CHART

1 – Black
2 – Yellow
3 – Gray
4 – Brown
5 – Green
6 – Blue

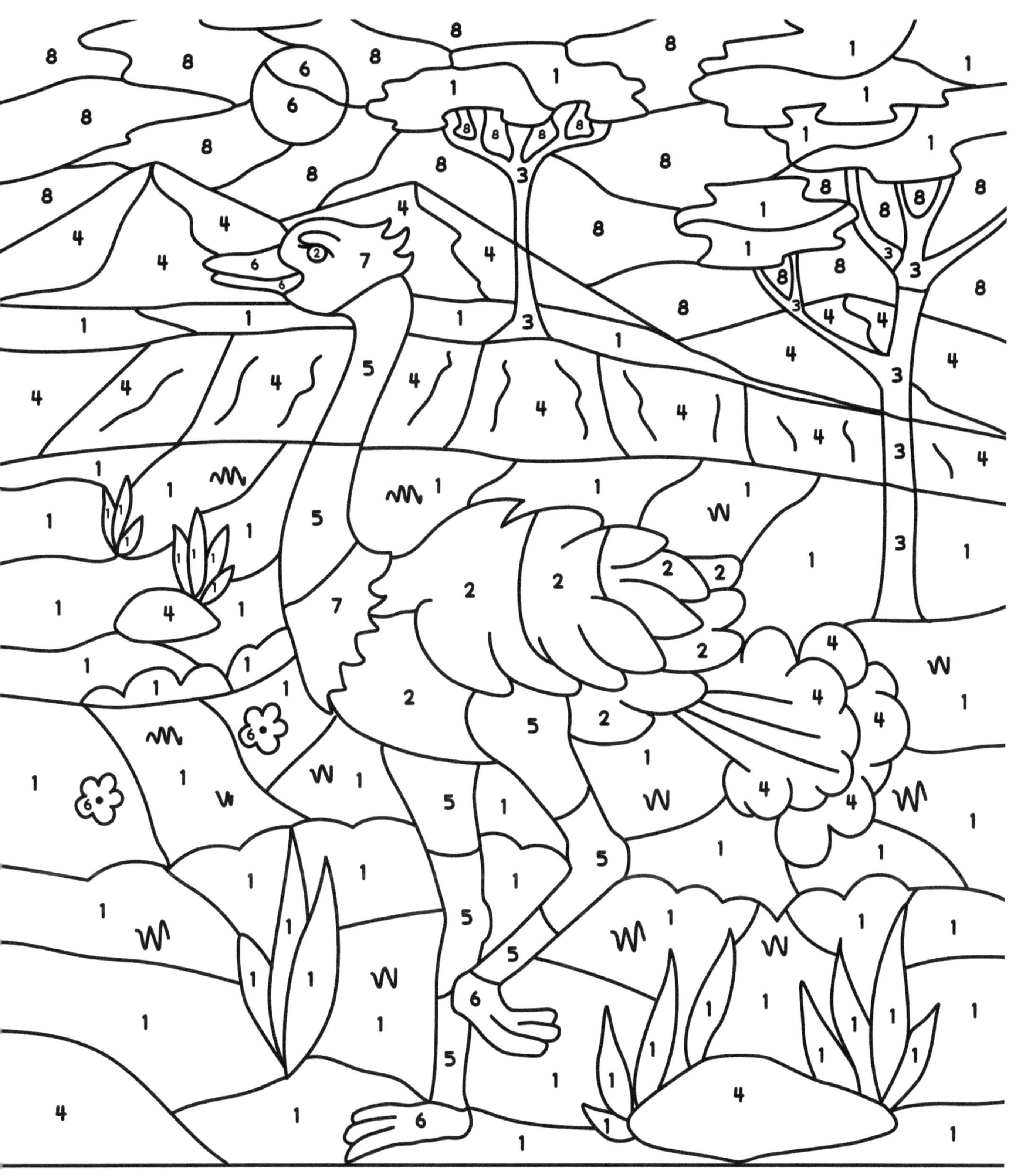

COLOR CHART

1 – Green
2 – Black
3 – Brown
4 – Gray
5 – Pink
6 – Orange
7 – White
8 – Blue

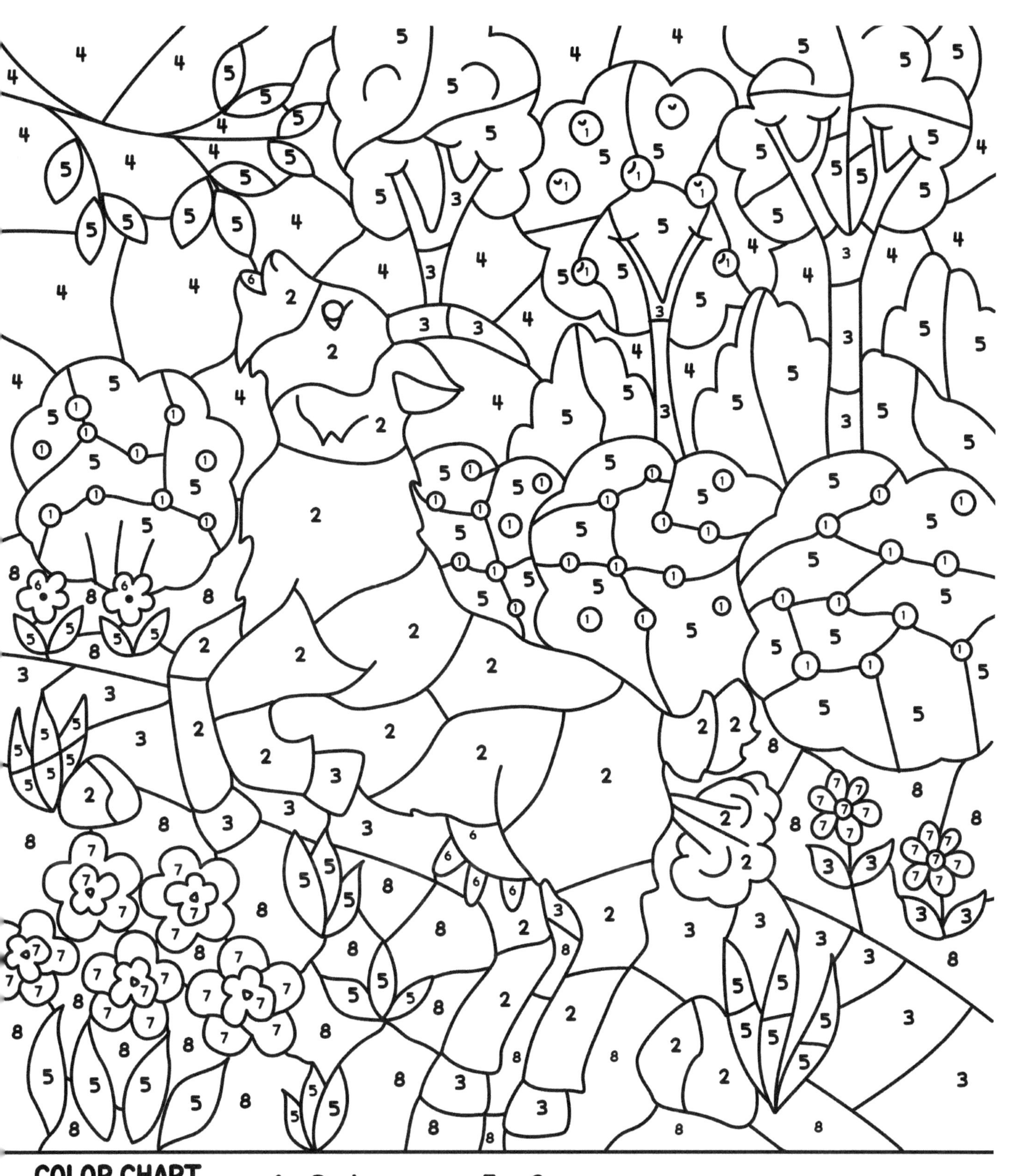

COLOR CHART

1 – Red
2 – Gray
3 – Brown
4 – Blue
5 – Green
6 – Pink
7 – Orange
8 – Dark Green

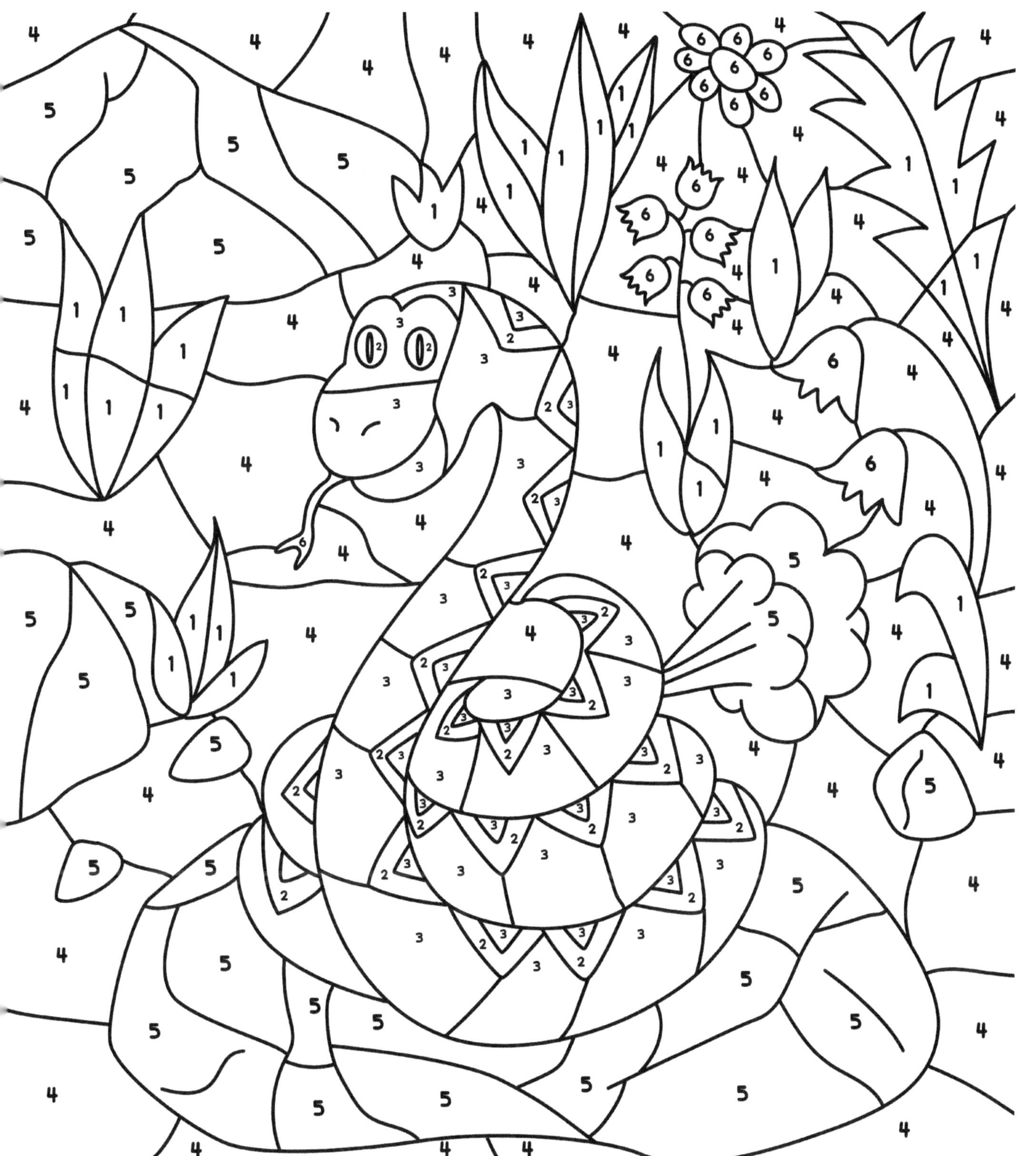

COLOR CHART

1 – Green
2 – Yellow
3 – Green
4 – Brown
5 – Gray
6 – Red

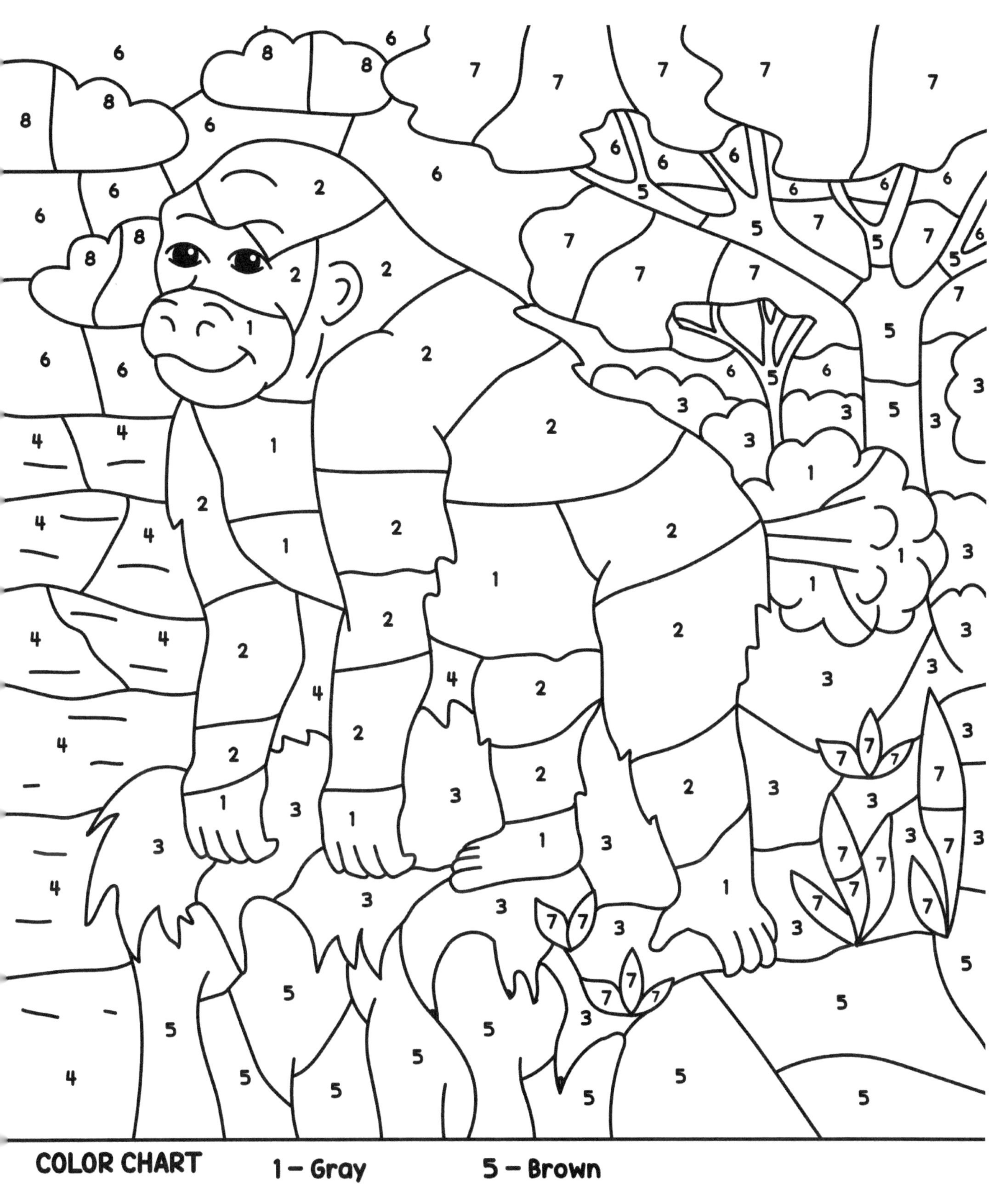

COLOR CHART

1 – Gray
2 – Black
3 – Green
4 – Dark Blue
5 – Brown
6 – Light Blue
7 – Dark Green
8 – White

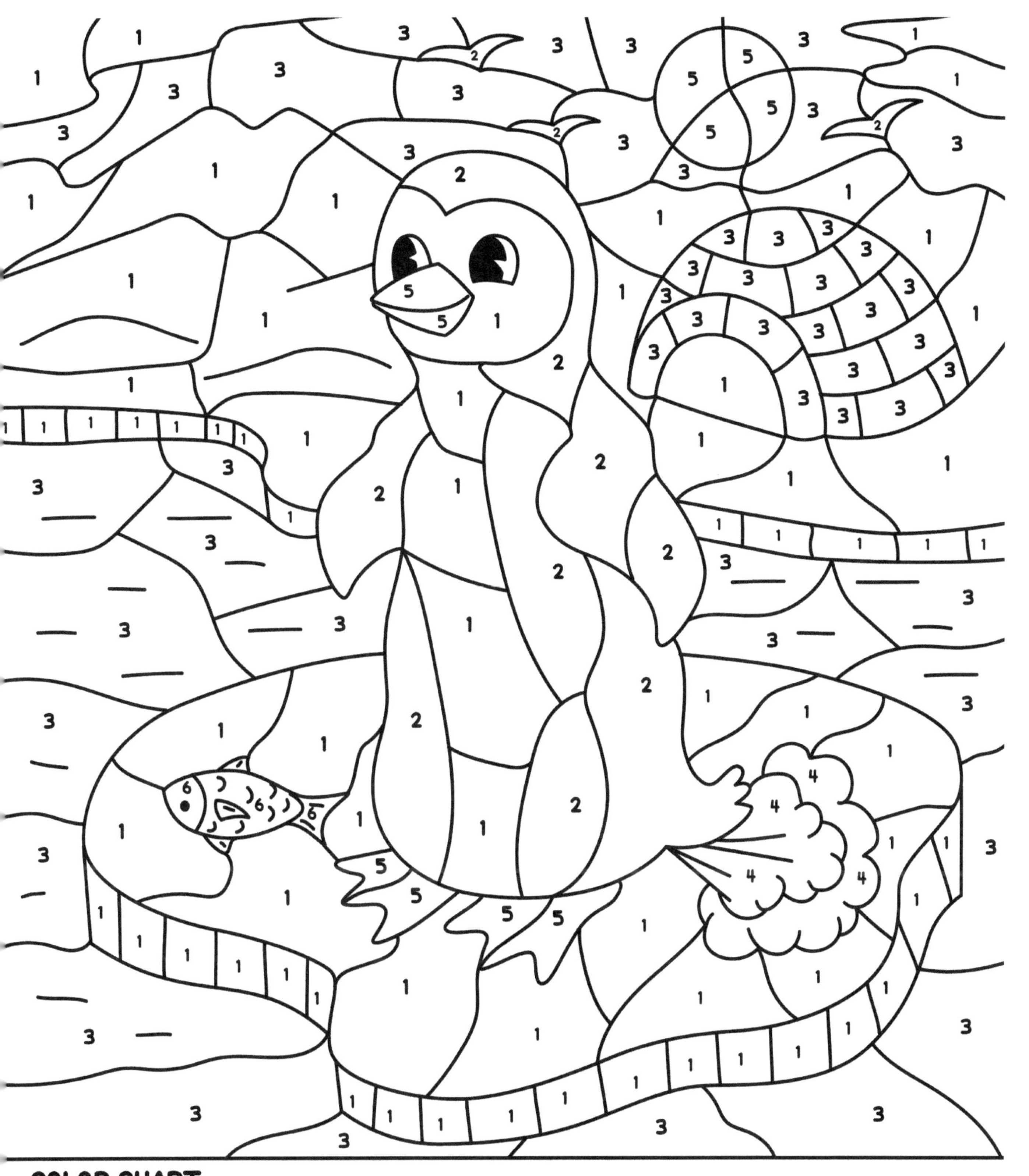

COLOR CHART

1 – White
2 – Black
3 – Blue
4 – Gray
5 – Orange
6 – Red

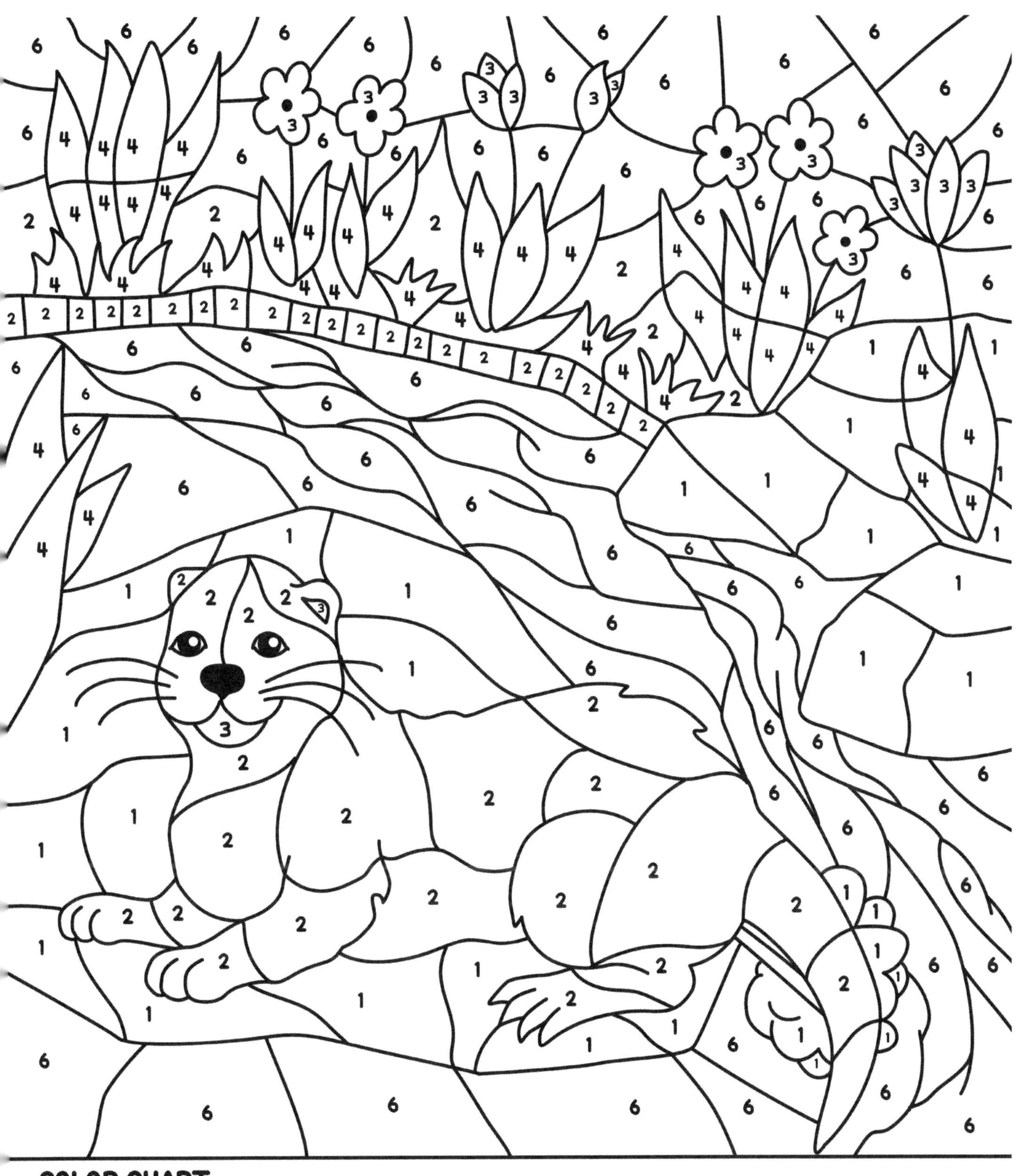

COLOR CHART

1 – Gray
2 – Brown
3 – Pink
4 – Green
5 – Tan
6 – Blue

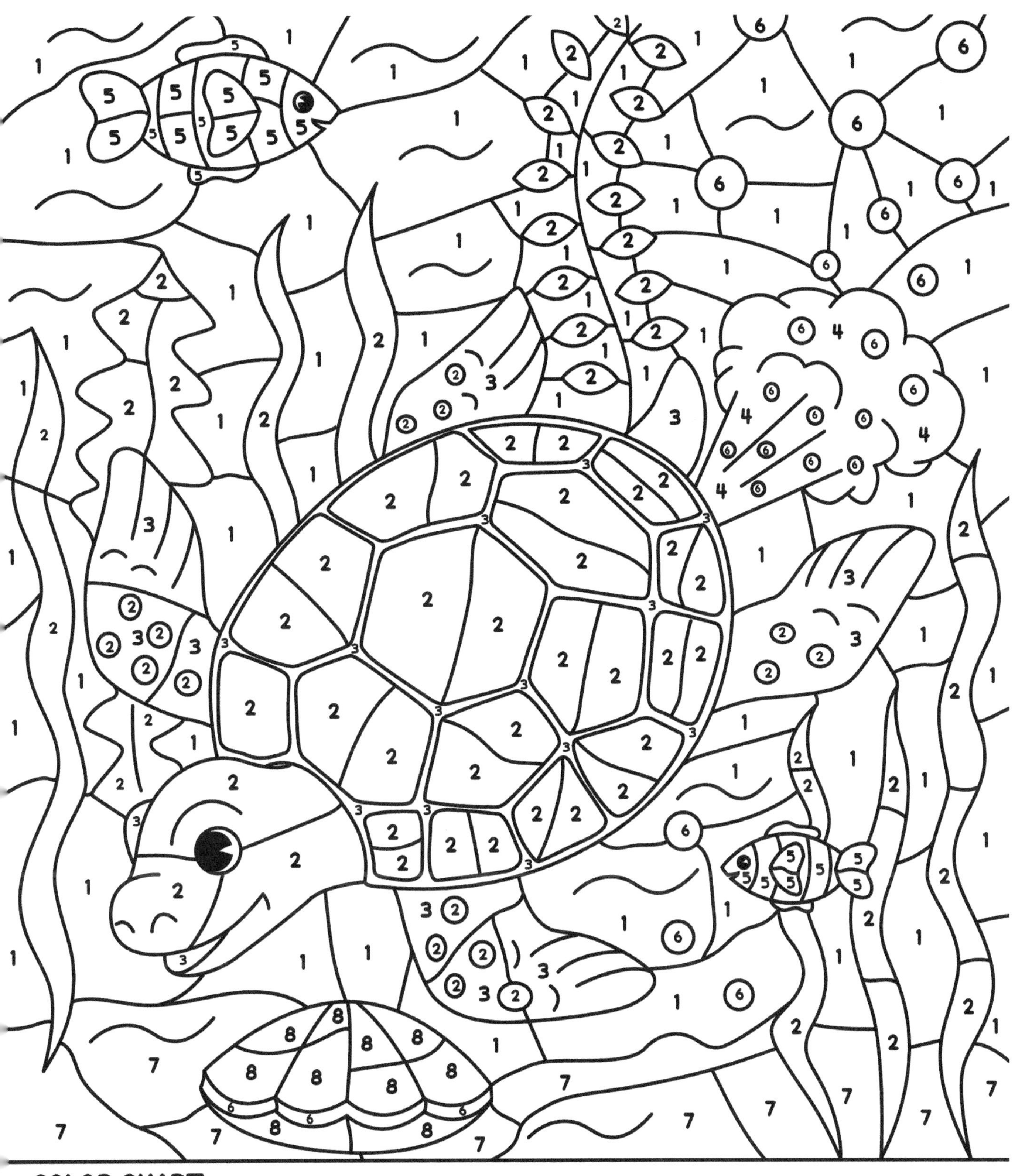

COLOR CHART

1 – Dark Blue	5 – Orange
2 – Green	6 – Light Blue
3 – Dark Green	7 – Tan
4 – Gray	8 – Purple

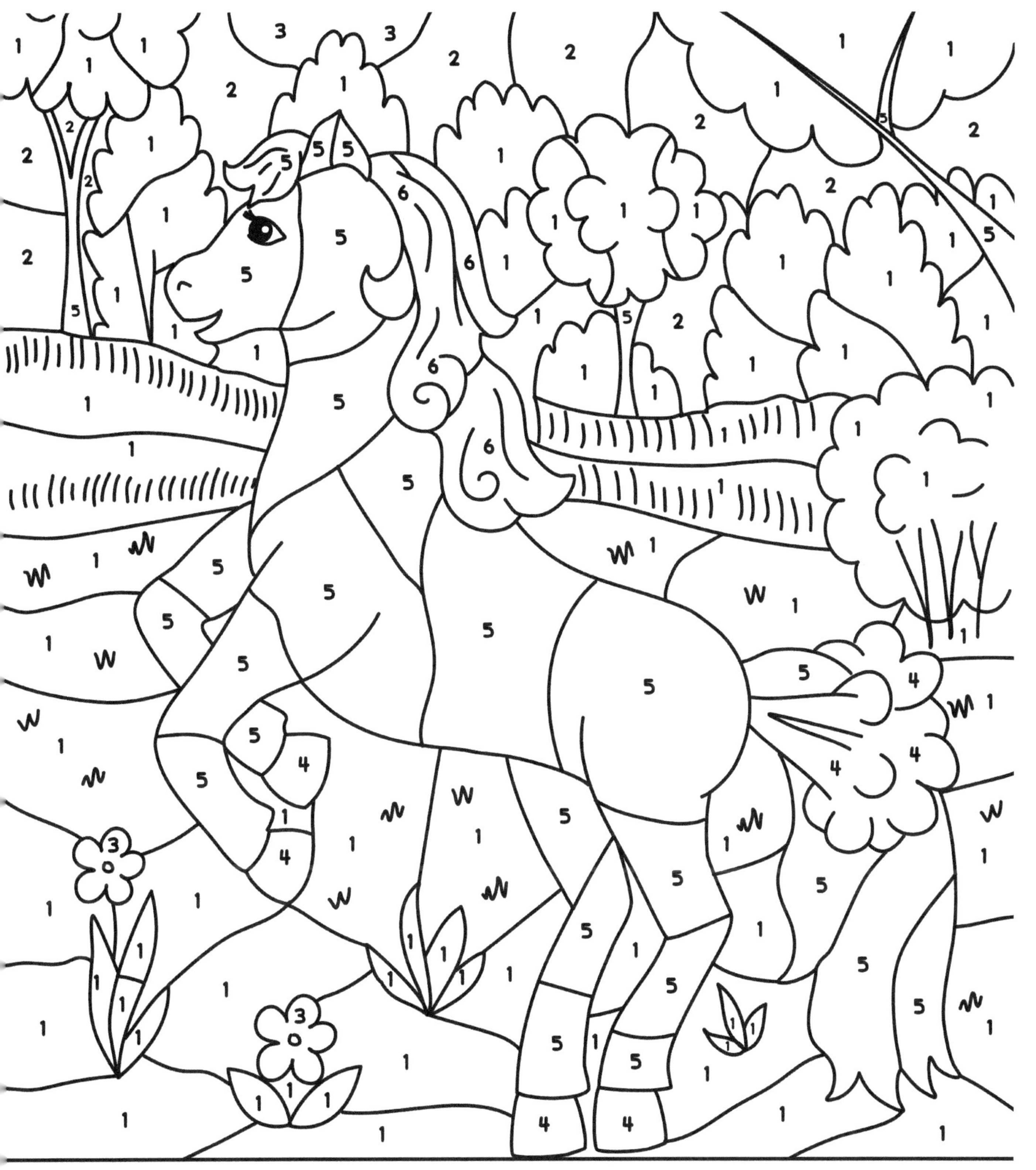

COLOR CHART

1 – Green
2 – Blue
3 – Yellow
4 – Gray
5 – Brown
6 – Black

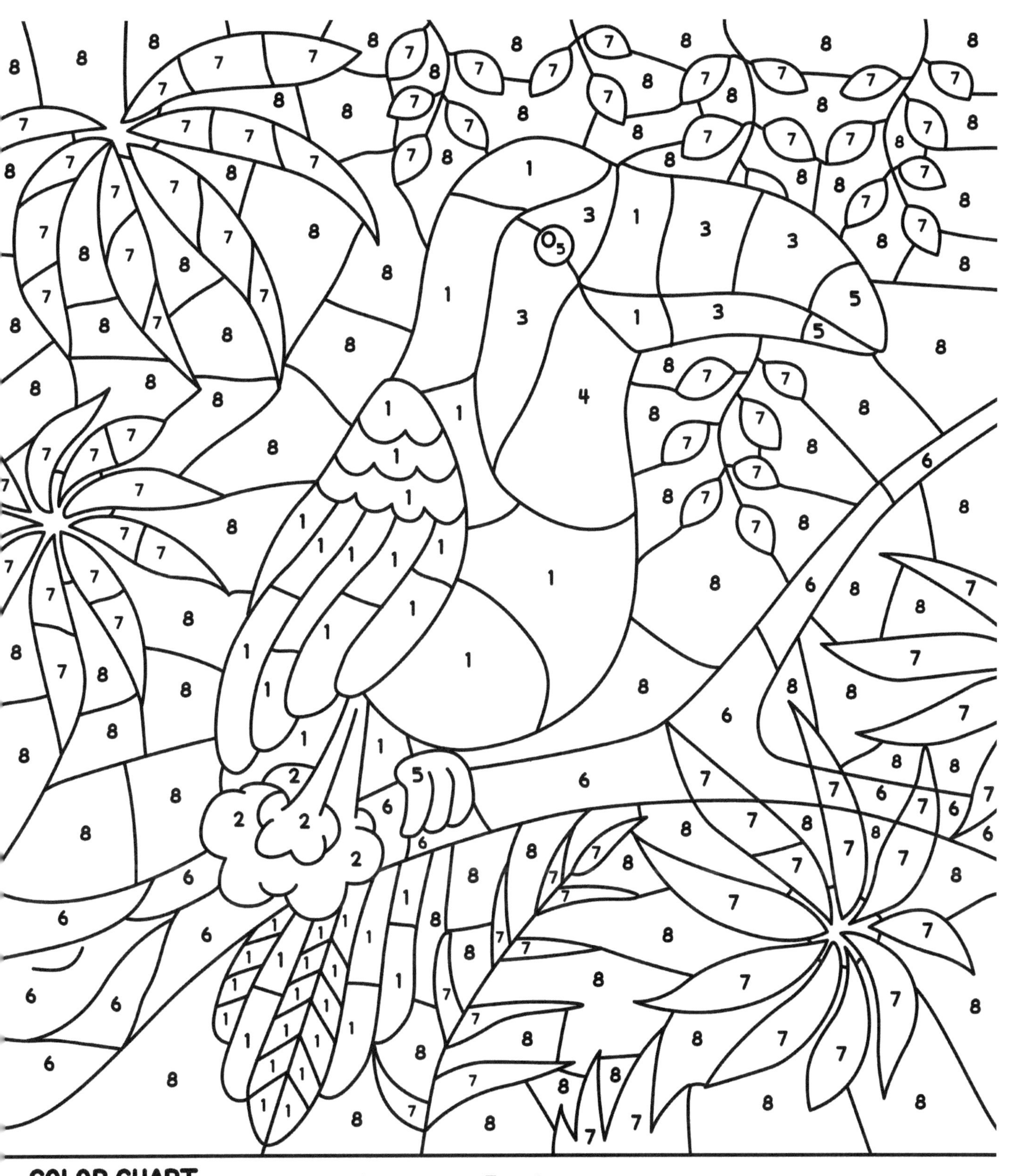

COLOR CHART

1 – Black
2 – Gray
3 – Yellow
4 – White
5 – Orange
6 – Brown
7 – Green
8 – Blue

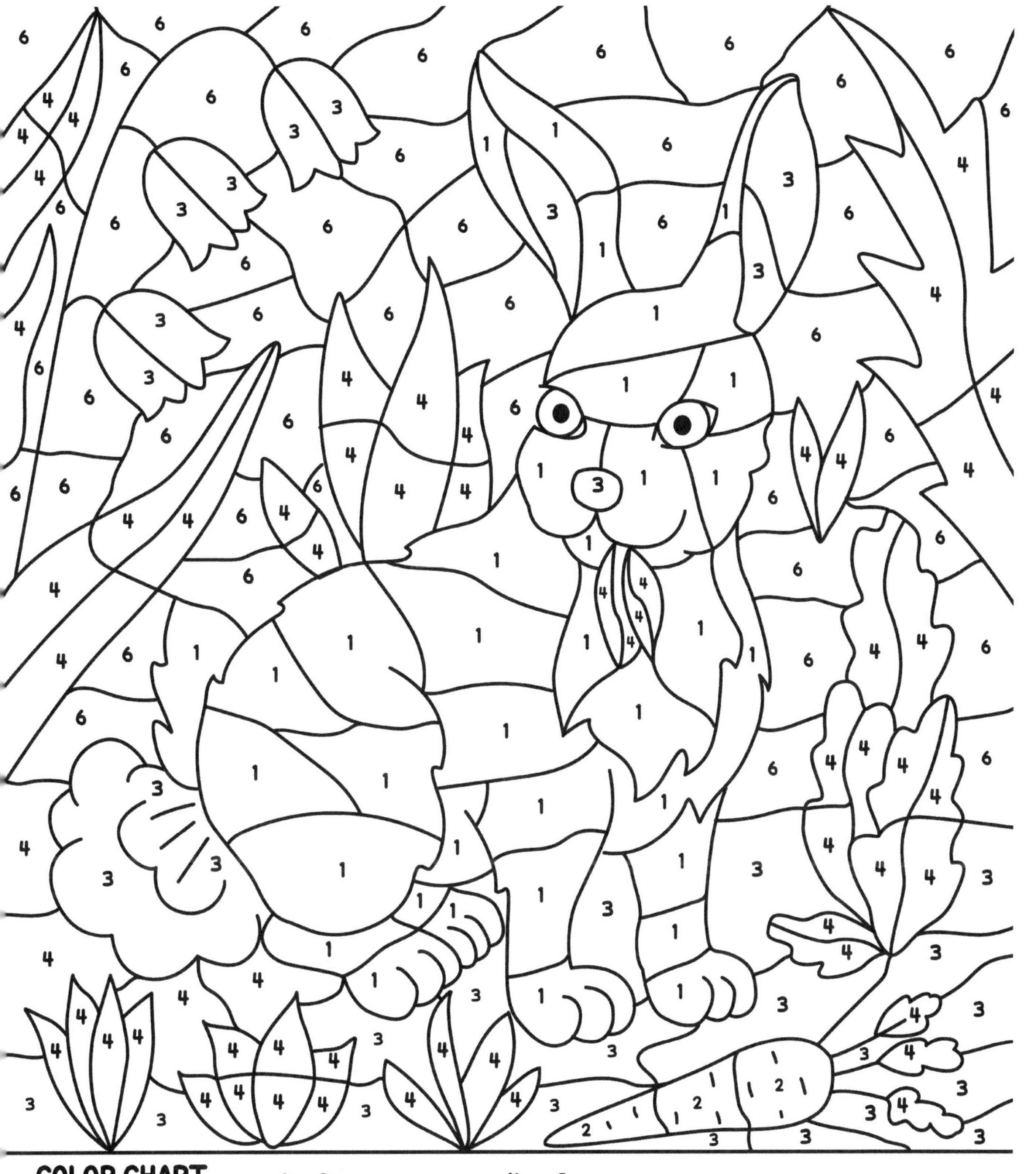

COLOR CHART

1 – Brown
2 – Orange
3 – Pink
4 – Green
5 – Gray
6 – Blue

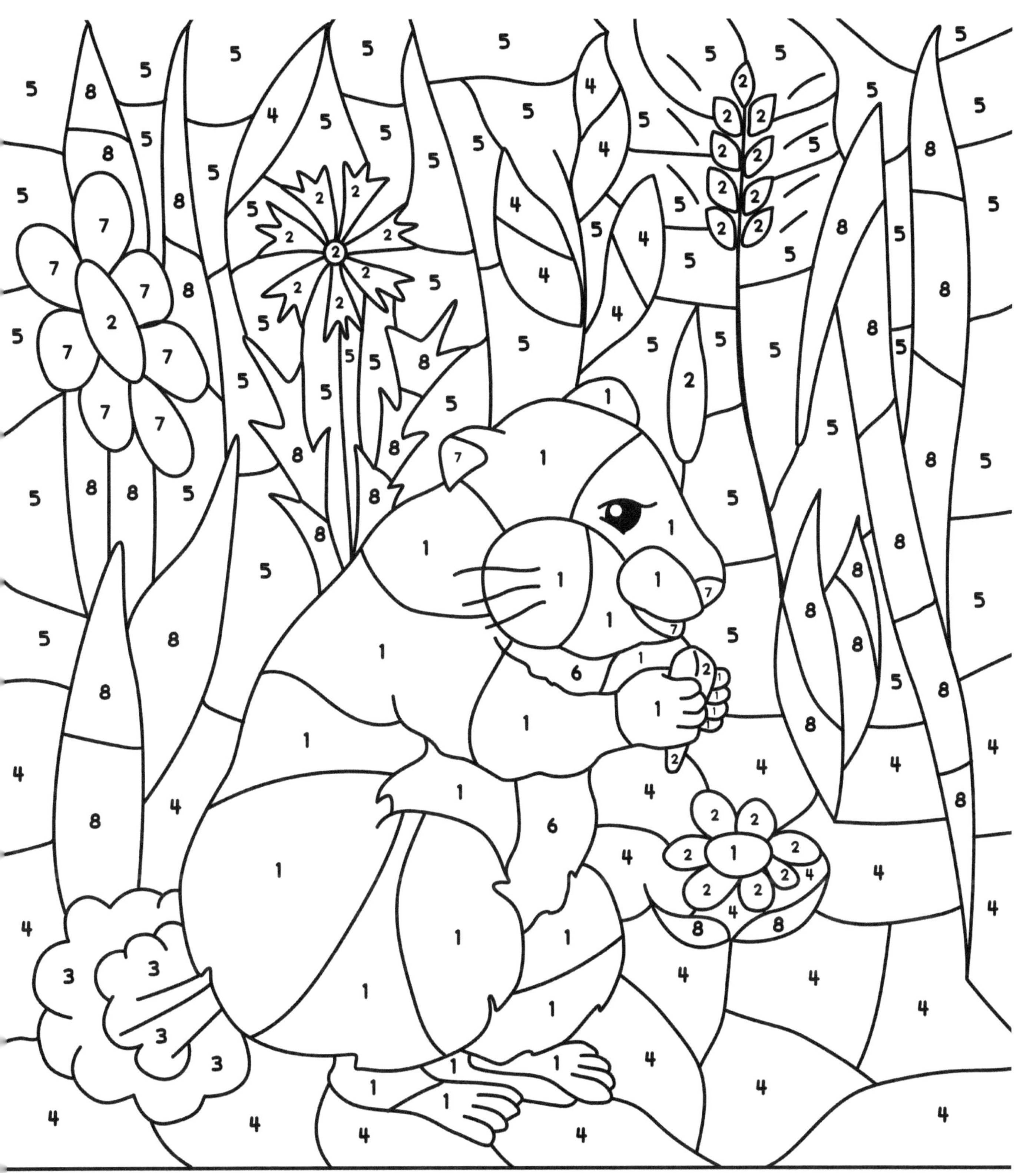

COLOR CHART

1 – Brown
2 – Yellow
3 – Gray
4 – Green
5 – Blue
6 – White
7 – Pink
8 – Dark Green

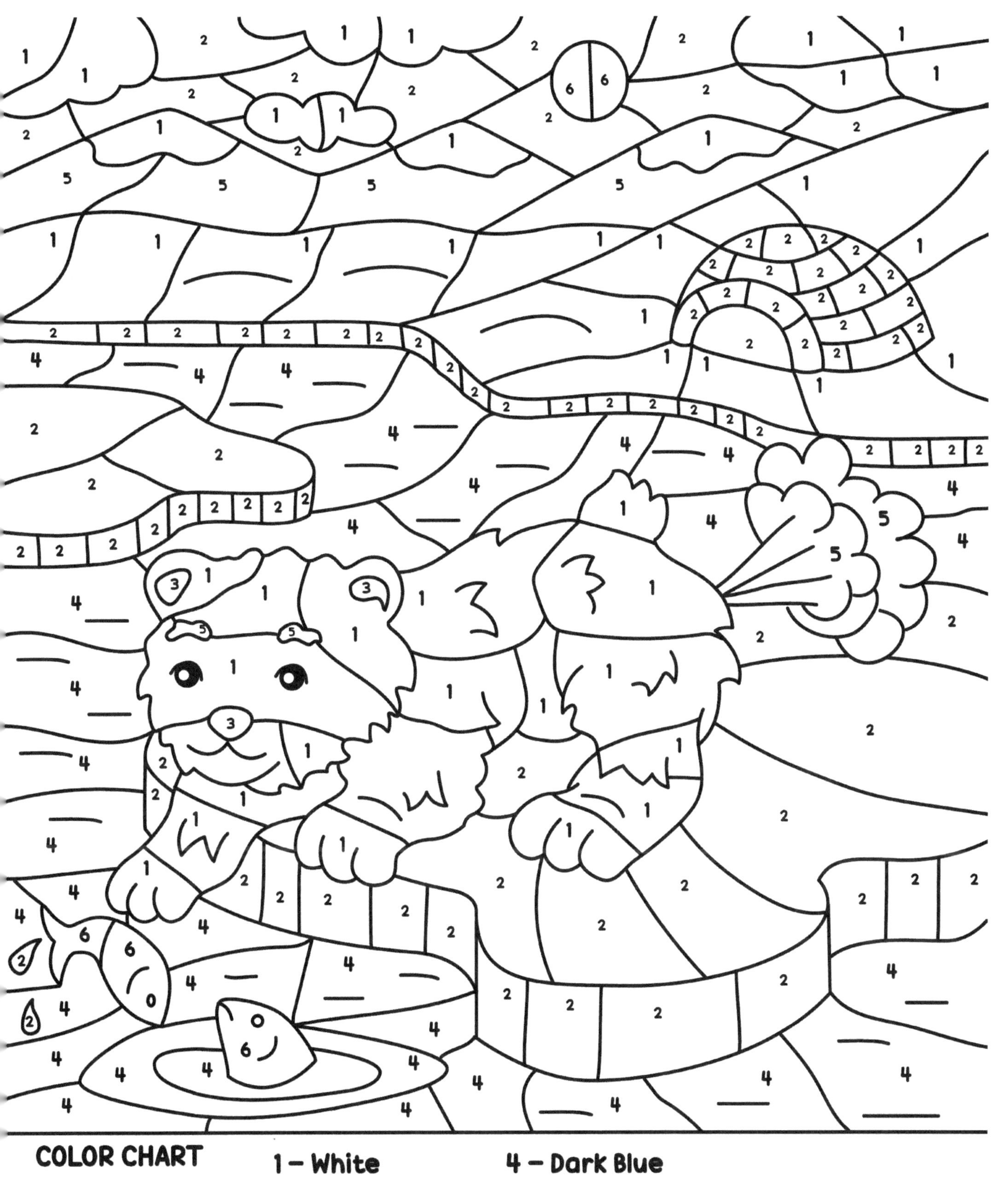

COLOR CHART

1 – White
2 – Light Blue
3 – Pink
4 – Dark Blue
5 – Gray
6 – Orange

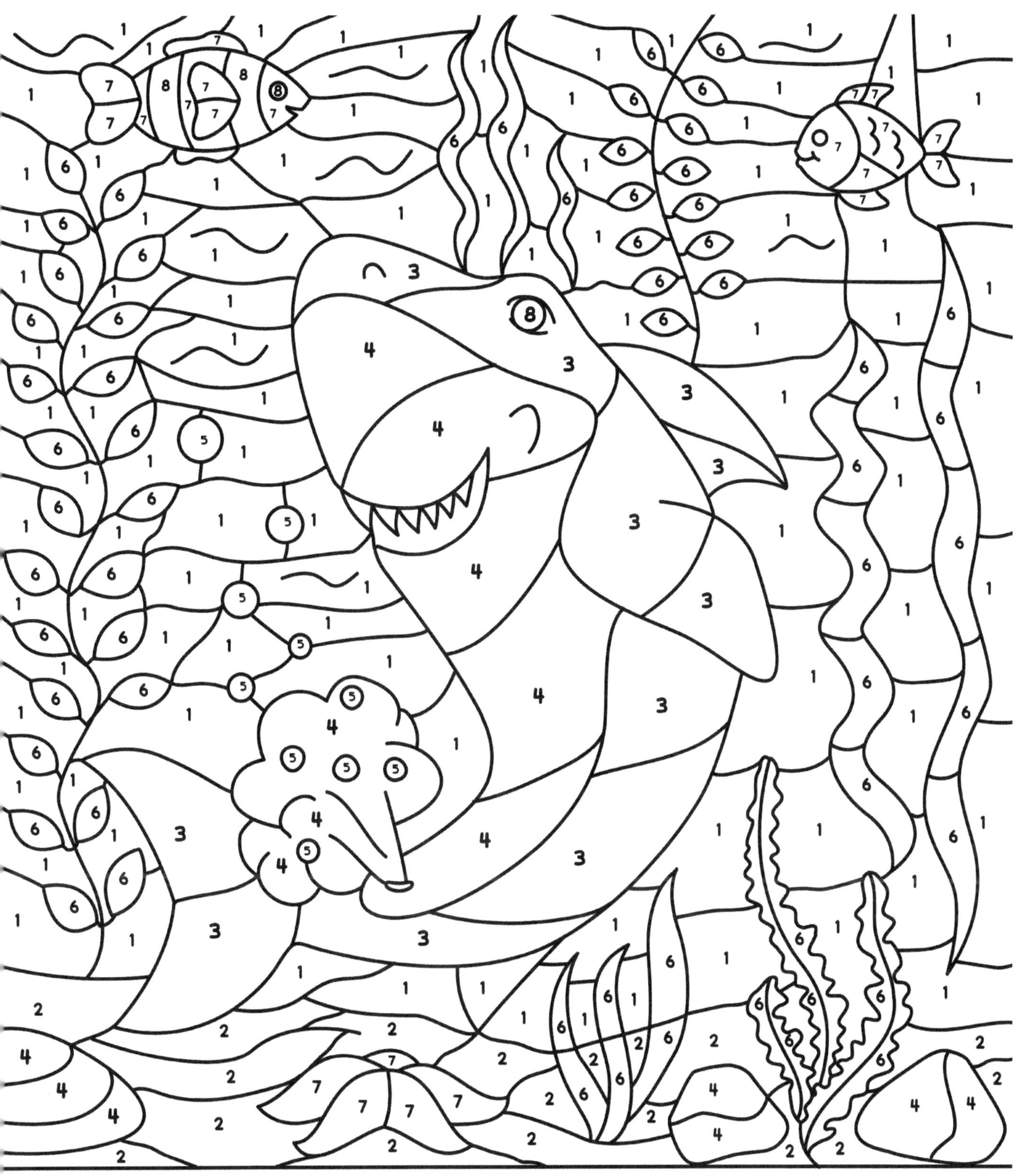

COLOR CHART

1 – Dark Blue	5 – Light Blue
2 – Tan	6 – Green
3 – Charcoal	7 – Orange
4 – Gray	8 – Black

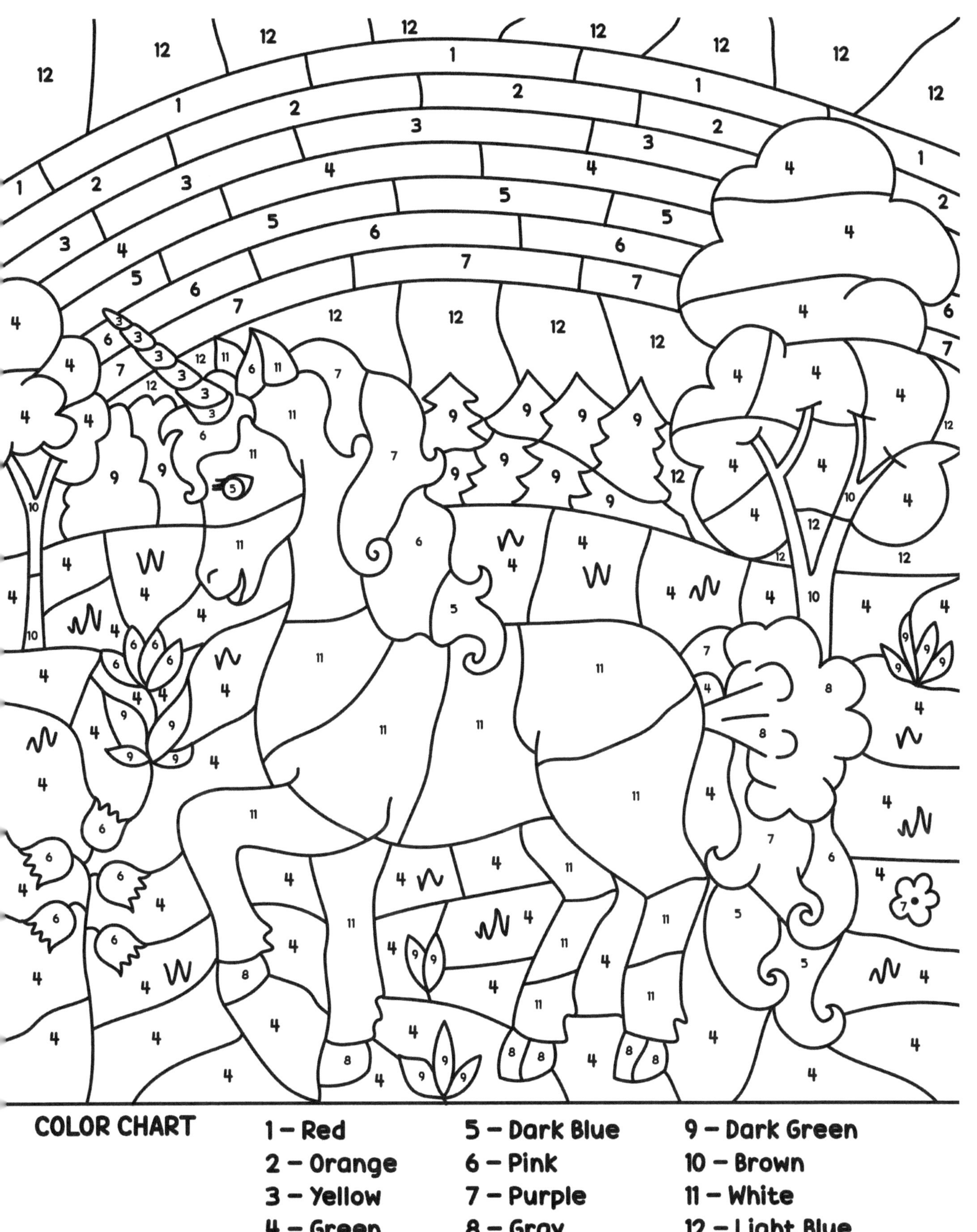
COLOR CHART
1 – Red
2 – Orange
3 – Yellow
4 – Green
5 – Dark Blue
6 – Pink
7 – Purple
8 – Gray
9 – Dark Green
10 – Brown
11 – White
12 – Light Blue

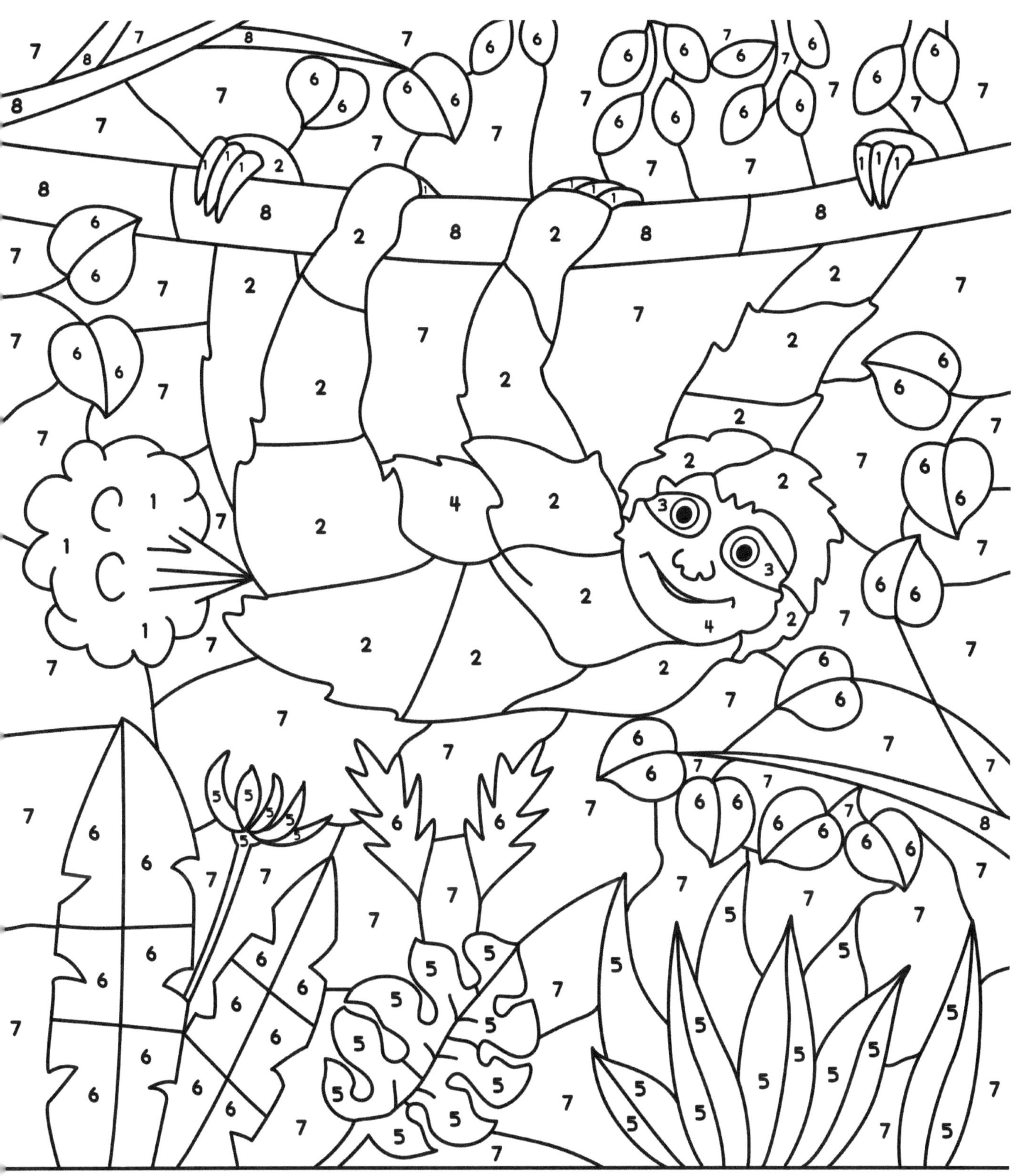

COLOR CHART

1 – Gray
2 – Tan
3 – Black
4 – White
5 – Green
6 – Dark Green
7 – Blue
8 – Brown

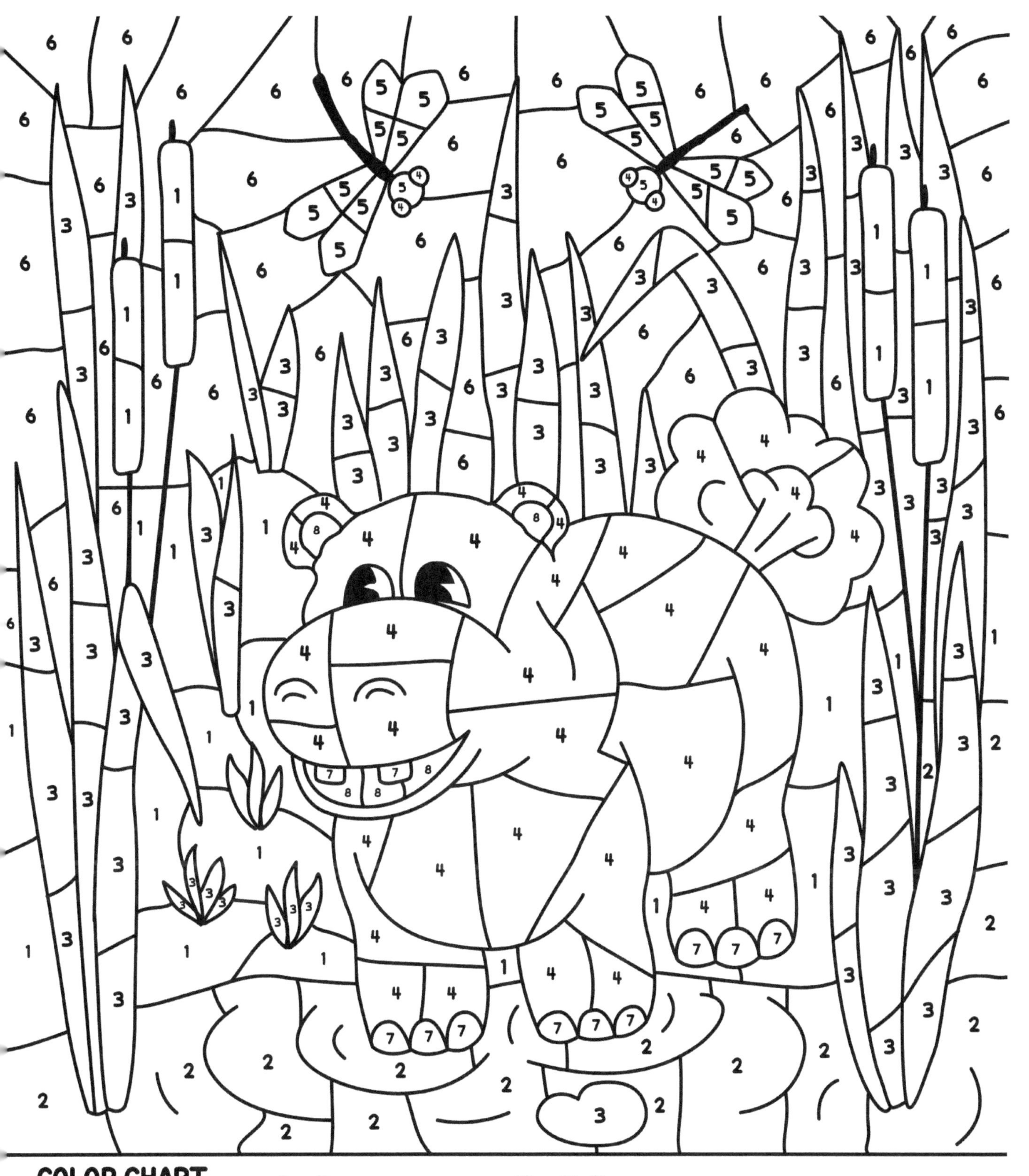

COLOR CHART

1 – Brown
2 – Dark Blue
3 – Green
4 – Gray
5 – Yellow
6 – Light Blue
7 – White
8 – Pink

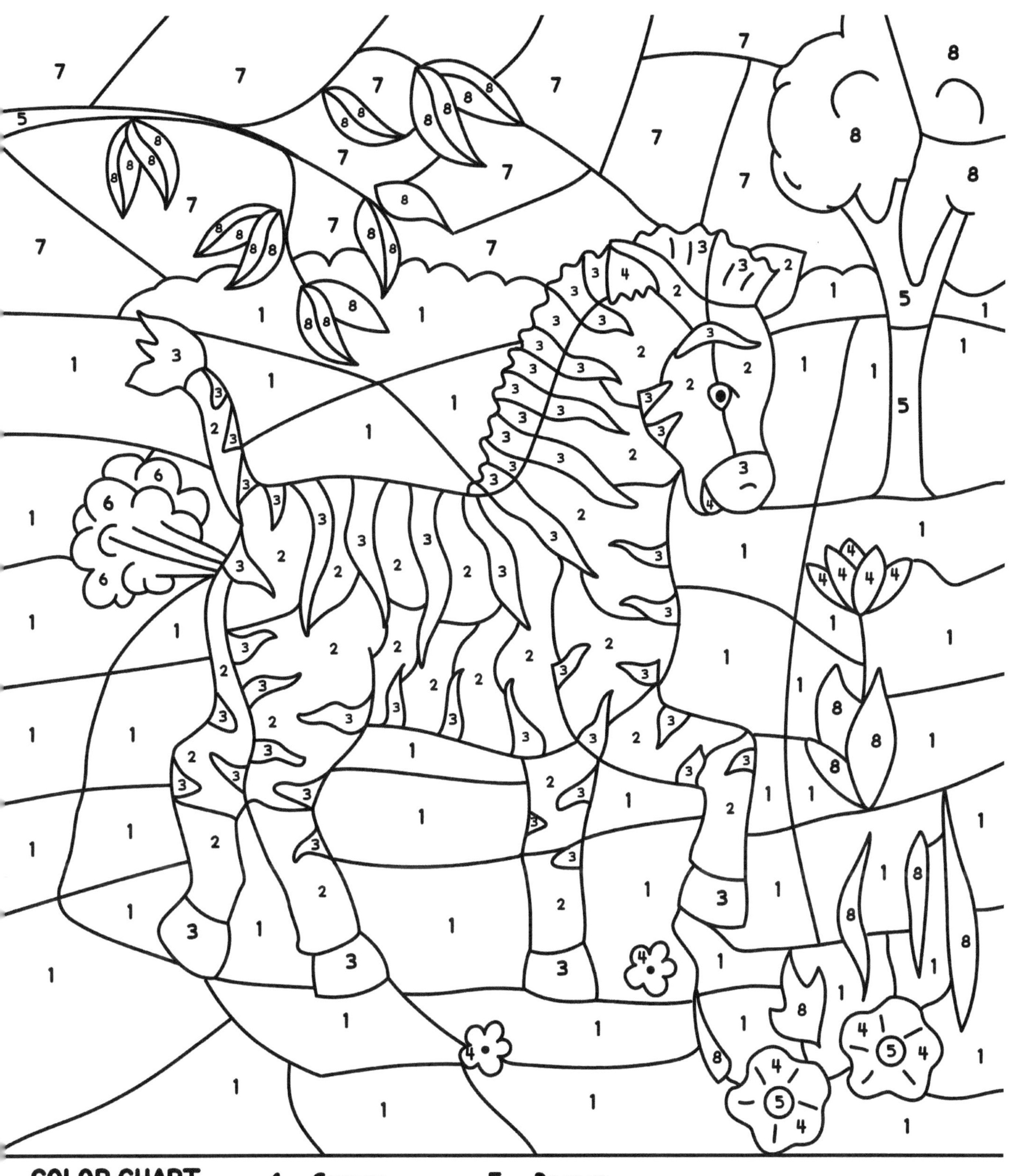

COLOR CHART

1 – Green
2 – White
3 – Black
4 – Pink
5 – Brown
6 – Gray
7 – Blue
8 – Dark Green

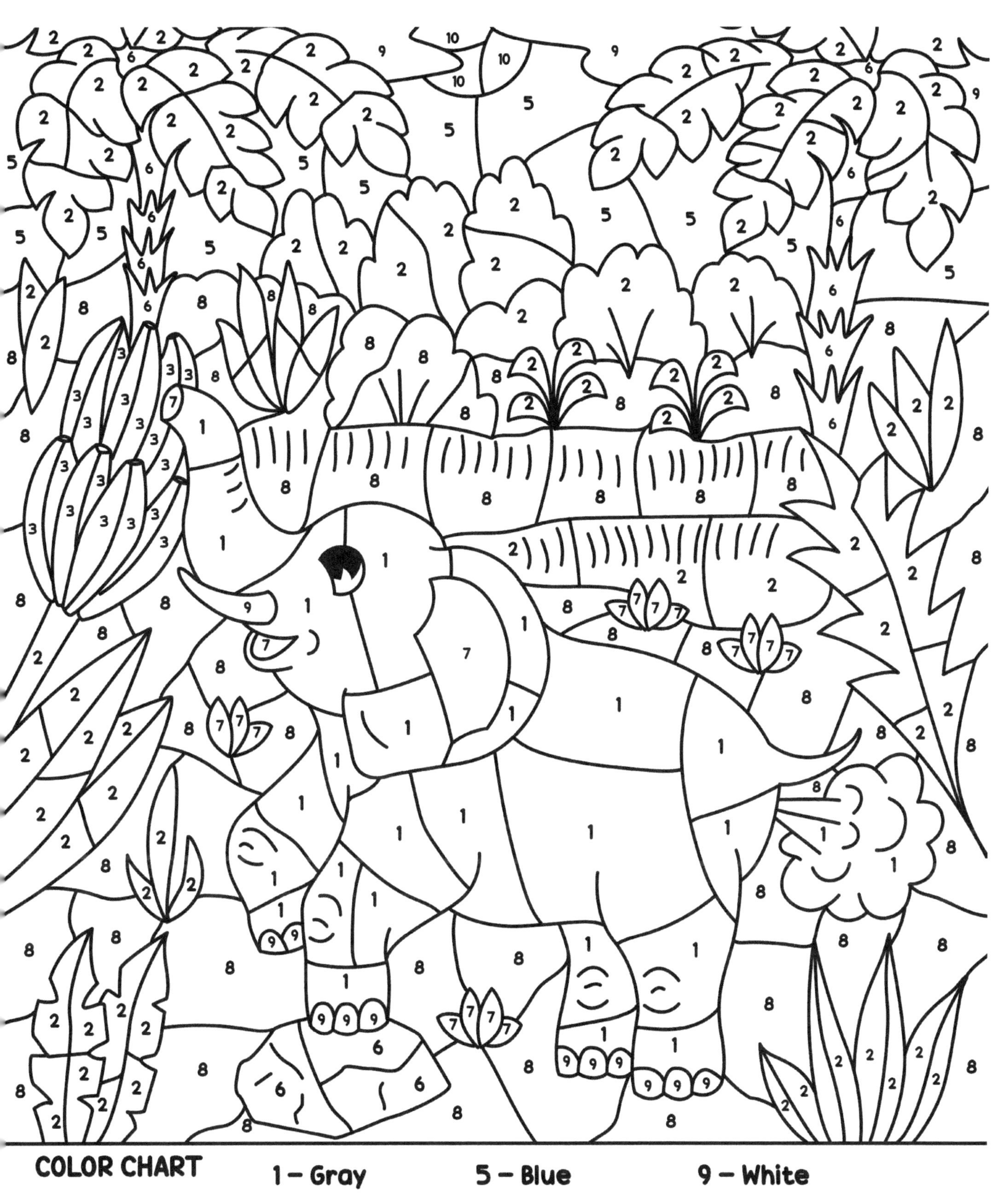

COLOR CHART

1 – Gray	5 – Blue	9 – White
2 – Green	6 – Brown	10 – Orange
3 – Yellow	7 – Pink	
4 – Purple	8 – Light Green	

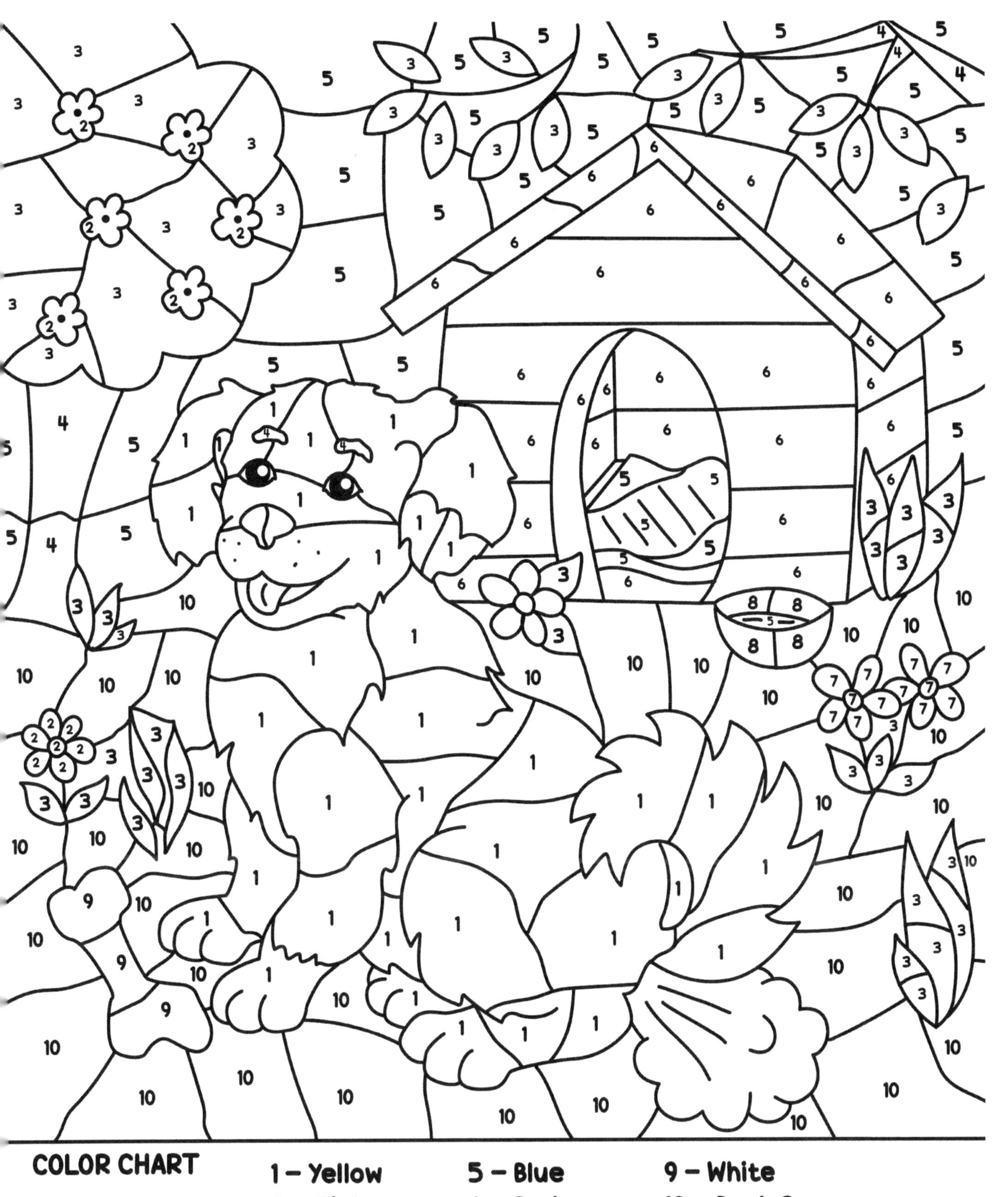

COLOR CHART

1 – Yellow	5 – Blue	9 – White
2 – Pink	6 – Red	10 – Dark Green
3 – Green	7 – Purple	
4 – Brown	8 – Gray	

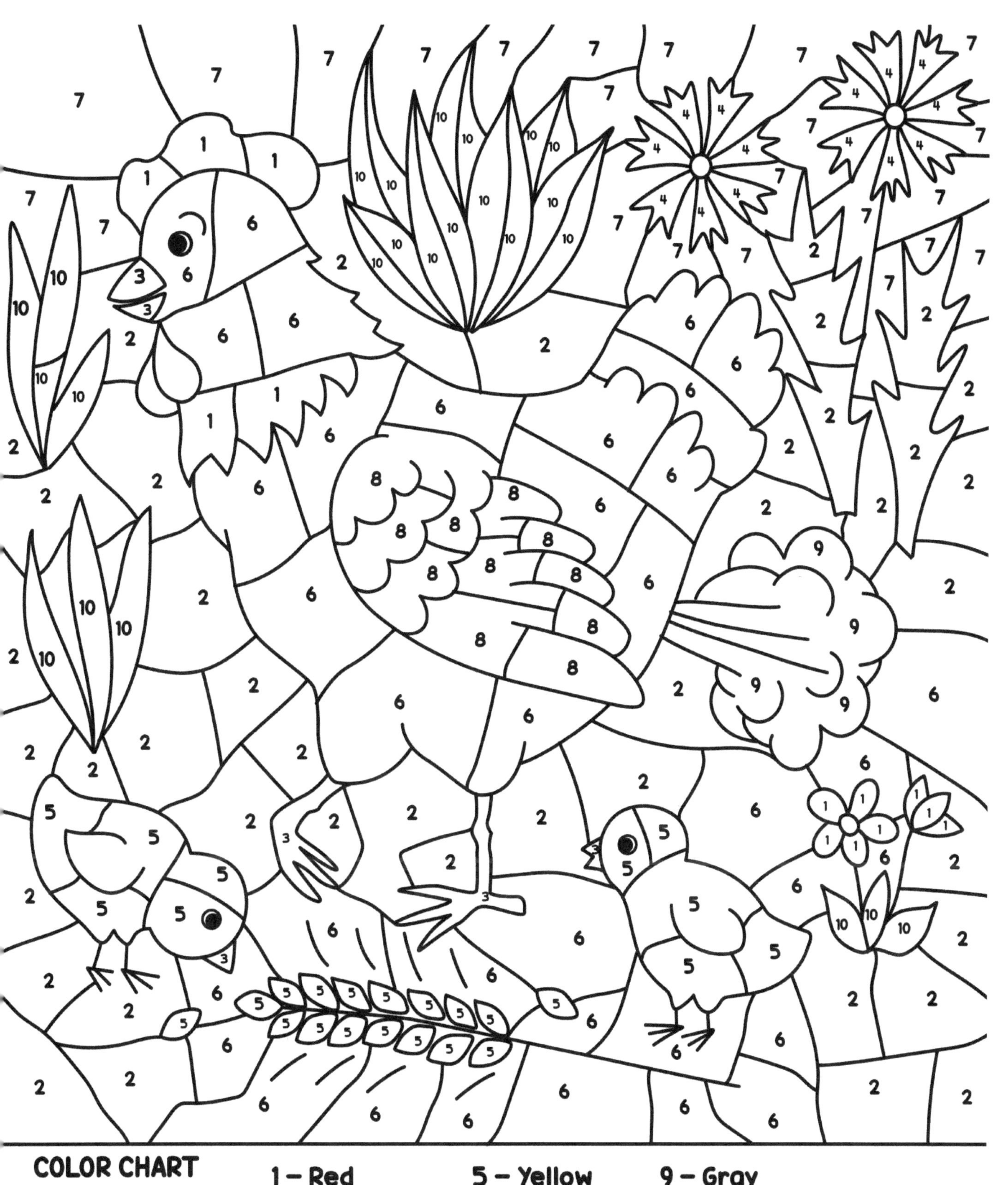

COLOR CHART

1 – Red
2 – Green
3 – Orange
4 – Purple
5 – Yellow
6 – Tan
7 – Blue
8 – Brown
9 – Gray
10 – Dark Green

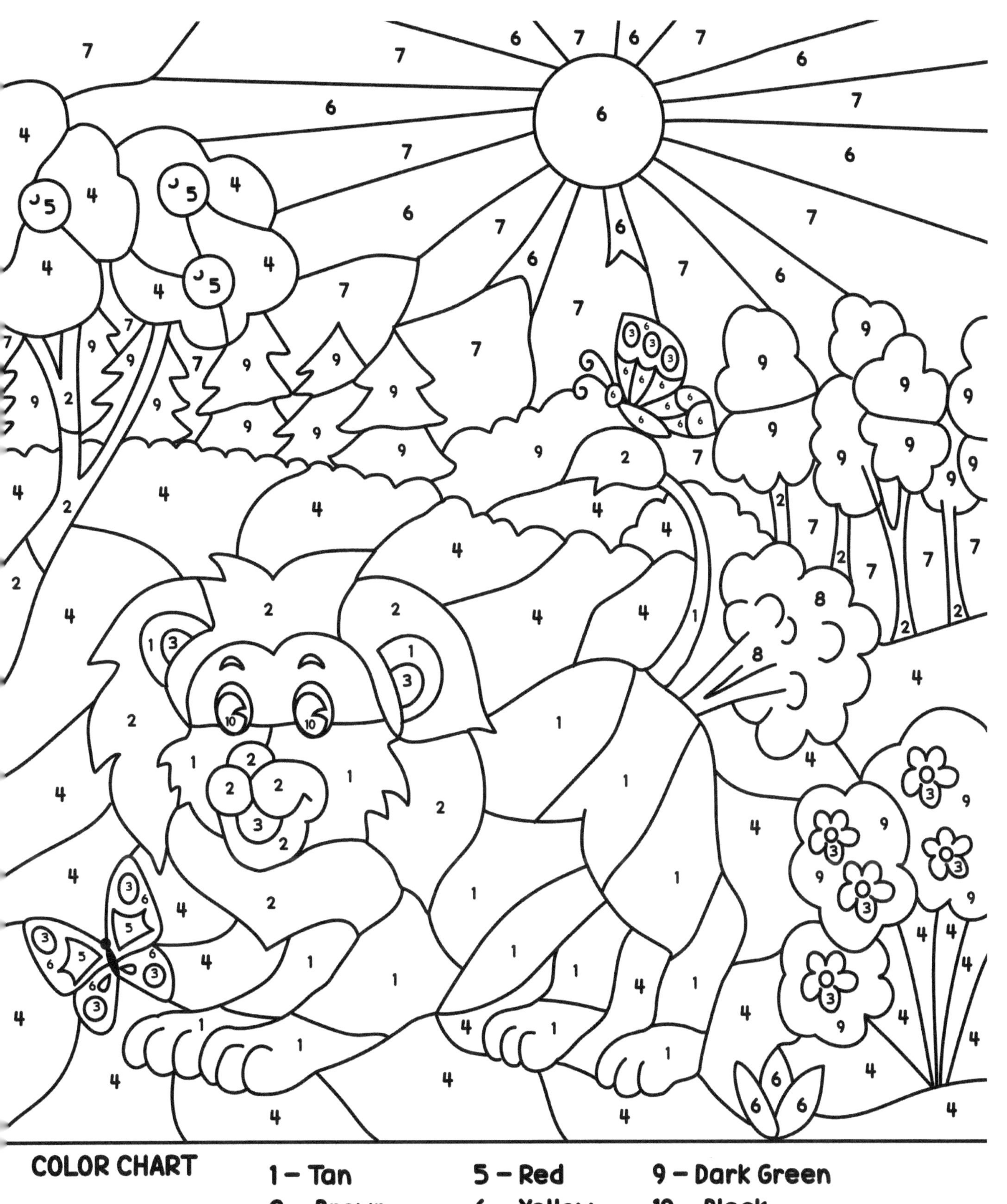

COLOR CHART

1 – Tan	5 – Red	9 – Dark Green
2 – Brown	6 – Yellow	10 – Black
3 – Pink	7 – Blue	
4 – Green	8 – Gray	

www.ingramcontent.com/pod-product-compliance
Lightning Source LLC
LaVergne TN
LVHW081301100826
845148LV00005B/944

* 9 7 8 1 6 4 9 4 3 0 6 5 6 *